The Way for Mankind

Book 1

Jean-Marie PAGLIA

The Way for Mankind

Book 1, Philosophical Intimations on Economic and Social Issues

JMP PUBLISHING

JMP Publishing
04170 Thorame Basse. France

ISBN : 978-2-9537218-1-2

www.thewayformankind.com

Acknowledgments

We would like to express our gratitude to all the authors directly or indirectly quoted in this book, in particular Anup Shah, Betsy Bowman and Bob Stone, Frank Brunner, Fritjof Capra, Paul Hawken, John Ikerd, Mila Kahlon, David Loy, Ethan Miller, and Venerable Payutto.

Their points of view help us understand the world.

Thanks, too, to Jacqueline Enjalbert for her illustrations.

This work is dedicated to those who are not put off by somewhat dry reading matter, and who savor the satisfaction of in-depth reflection.

Foreword

In the times we live in, most of us must seriously be wondering about the way the human race is going. We are faced with a mound of major problems for which we seem to have no solution, and there seems to be no articulated or agreed idea for defining our way forward, as though we were steadily and resolutely moving towards our goal, without having any goal whatsoever.

The following pages express the bewilderment and the reflections of the common man; not an expert, and not someone who is ever consulted. Nevertheless, the ordinary man thinks, gathers information and listens to many different points of view because he would very much like to understand, and shape his own destiny accordingly. Let us enter his thoughts, follow them and develop them, for they are your thoughts – our thoughts - and we may be surprised at how similar our ideas turn out to be. The thoughts expressed here come from all kinds of different horizons and are addressed to every person living on this Earth. But we will have to be brave to go all the way, for the road ahead is arduous.

Let's take a look at where we stand now, tracing the thoughts of those who have been observing the world's problems.

First of all, in this volume, let's examine the situation in economic and social terms.

What do we see?

1. A Quick Glance at the Planet

Let's look at Mumbai. Here are a few details from an article in *Le Monde Diplomatique* : "India's City of Gold." (1)

> "Many slum dwellers have built two or three lofts atop their hovels and rented them out. On average 10 people live in a single hut of about nine square meters. No one can estimate how many people live on Reay Road, but every single day the headcount increases and with it the chaos. To be honest, no one can even confirm how many people live in the city overall. Official surveys show that there are 12 million (more than Greece) and that half of them are homeless. But because of the endless stream of immigrants, the slum population, the hundreds of unregistered children born every day, it may be closer to 16 million [...]
>
> Many have come from far to settle in the City of Hope, convinced they would find jobs [...] So they survive here, on the road, day after day, despite the pollution, heat, malnutrition, dirt, trucks and cars whizzing by, accidents, diseases, huge rats and crows, stinking gutters, the disgust of better-off passers-by and the monsoon floods [...]
>
> It takes a while to realize why it continues to attract so many outsiders who hope to make their fortunes here. It is overwhelmingly huge, hot, cramped, polluted, suffocating, crowded, traffic-choked, with appalling sights and smells of poverty and sickness. If you are poor, you live in inhuman conditions; if you are rich, the mafia bothers you. If you are middle-class, just leaving your house every morning is a

struggle - fighting with traffic, negotiating potholes, trying to ignore tiny begging hands scratching your car windows."

This account could equally well describe hundreds of cities around the world. It is evidence of the sorry state of our planet.

We are regularly kept abreast of the general state of the world. Here are a few examples from websites keeping an eye on the world's problems - there are many sources of information at our disposal. Most of the figures quoted in this chapter come from the *Global Issues* website (2), which offers a very thorough analysis of the social, economic and political problems affecting our planet. Here is a brief rundown of the overall situation, a reality far easier to contemplate when it's reduced to statistics:

Two billion people suffer from malnutrition, and 18 million starve to death every year.

Millions of people die each year from curable or preventable diseases.

1.3 billion people have no access to drinking water; 3 billion have no sanitation and 2 billion do not have electricity.

Poverty, hunger, malnutrition, disease, appalling sanitation and illiteracy haunt a large proportion of the world's population. We could flesh out the description of this world of ours by mentioning child labor (25 million children are exploited in unacceptable working conditions), the terrible conditions for many women and the lack of respect for basic human rights.

It would be interesting to try and understand how we have managed to make such a mess of our existence and our dignity.

We human beings are real idiots.

The genesis of this global tragedy is largely the result of clashes between cultures. Over the last few centuries, Europe's aggressive, mercantile cultures came into contact with peaceful subsistence economies. As we all know, these encounters were not harmonious – you only have to think about Conquistadors seizing gold, land, souls and people in the newly discovered "Indies", or the slave trade - the buying and selling of human "ebony". Cultural differences were too great to give rise to fair exchanges.

The tragedy of under-development appears to stem from those historical exchanges. Colonialism opened up vast territories that were exploited by rich countries. The colonized peoples found themselves in a state of economic inferiority, and they have remained in that state ever since.

Following the end of colonialism, strategic aspects of world trade have remained under the control of the dominant powers, notably thanks to gaining the allegiance of local elites.

It is the rich who decide upon trade regulations, shape international institutions and control information, and these trade advantages enable them to exploit resources for their own benefit, depriving the producing countries of their fare share.

Conditions imposed by international institutions upon poor countries maintain their dependence and under-development, as they favor trade which does not benefit the poorer countries.

Poor nations can no longer produce their own food and do not have the means to develop their own industries.

Free trade does not equal fair trade. Wealth continues to be transferred from poor countries to rich countries, and the weakest countries are forced to accept unfair deals.

What's more, rich countries know how to protect themselves from imports which could harm their economies.

Poor countries urgently require investment in the areas of infrastructure, education and health before being able to establish fair trading conditions, but their efforts for self-development are crushed by the burden of debt, some of which dates back to colonial times.

A number of cause-and-effect relationships bind the two extremes of this human imbalance, and such bonds are rarely brought to light. Let's examine debt as one such example.

Nations emerging from colonization started out indebted to their former colonial masters during the 1960s, and the debt has continued to grow ever since. Borrowed billions find their way back to the rich countries, which become even richer from this exchange. "The poor are subsidizing the rich" as they say. Debt continues to increase with compound interest, reaching dizzying heights, and the vicious cycle can only be broken by canceling the debt.

According to the Jubilee 2000 report by the World Bank, debt continues to grow despite larger payments, while the amount of aid is decreasing. International aid is down 20% from the 1990s, and countries which pledged a defined percentage of their GNP in aid have not kept their word.

For every dollar received in the form of aid, the Third World pays back 13 dollars. The production of wealth required by these countries for their own development is being siphoned off - in the 1980s real income fell by 60% in Mexico, 50% in Argentina, and 70% in Peru.

It is fortunate that we are not aware of all this; it would make us uneasy. If we were aware of it, on the other hand, and were not overly concerned, we would have to admit that we are essentially self-engrossed creatures, conscious only of our own interests and concerns.

And it should also be remembered that in the poorest countries, the people who have to repay such debts did not contract them in the first place. They never saw the money at all.

Kofi Annan, Secretary General of the United Nations, pointed out during a conference on October 30, 2003, that in the previous year developing countries had paid almost 200 billion dollars to third countries.

> "Funds ought to be flowing from developed countries into developing countries, but the figures are telling us that the opposite is true. Funds which should be encouraging investment or growth in developing countries, or building schools and hospitals or supporting other measures for [...] development, are, on the contrary, moving abroad."

The United Nations development programme estimates that transfers from South to North are worth $500 billion per year, while aid donated to the Third World totals around $50 billion.

According to the economist Manfred Max-Neef, developing countries subsidize industrialized countries to the tune of hundreds of billions of dollars every year. Max-Neef calculates that around $400 billion net are transferred from Latin America to industrialized countries. (3)

Ten years after the World Food Summit, which pledged to reduce by half the number of people suffering from malnutrition by the year 2015, no progress has been recorded and 854 million people still do not have enough to eat, according to the FAO annual report on food insecurity (October 2006.)

The world is what we make of it, and what we make of it also shows who we are. It has to be said that we have not managed to make a very decent world, nor one which we should be happy about. However, we are not particularly concerned about it – to us, such problems appear insurmountable and remote.

2. Neoliberalism, the Principle of the Global Economic Order

The fundamental economic rules governing our planet are well known, and are laid down by the most powerful nations who thus ensure they can obtain the best for their national self-interest. Over time, economic principles have evolved to some extent, while naturally remaining basically the same.

The neoliberal theory is based upon the idea of the greatest possible economic freedom within a system of triumphant capitalism.

The fundamental principle of free trade sees in a totally free market a magic wand capable of providing all the benefits one could possibly hope for; freed from state intervention, excessive regulation, price controls and the weight of the unions, free trade spurs on the economy. The free movement of goods, services and capital generates sustained growth.

The privatization of public companies ensures that they are efficient and profitable.

Free trade develops global commerce and enables every country to develop in turn. It guarantees the most just and most efficient distribution of resources.

Competition gives the system magical energy – healthy competition between countries, companies and individuals within companies encourages the success of the best and stimulates innovation, lowers prices and gets the best results. This sacrosanct competition is at the very core of every personal preoccupation – it is an expression of the survival principle, the ancestral expression of human activity.

What could be better than that?

As far as we can judge, it would seem that this system has indeed brought inestimable progress in many areas. Notably, globalization has meant that emerging countries have been able to get off the ground economically, as outsourcing brings jobs there, even if this remains a form of exploitation.

Obviously, this kind of economic activity distributes a certain amount of wealth and improves living standards, but not in a way that is satisfactory, efficient or balanced. The undeniable proof right in front of us is the current state of the planet and also in long-since developed rich countries where economic disparities have not disappeared with time, but persist and are often getting worse - a sure sign that this revered free market economy is not functioning well at all.

This economic activity does not meet the needs of the people, as half of us remain completely impoverished while a fifth of us consume almost all the world's resources.

The article from *Global Issues*, "Primer on Neoliberalism" (1) notes that within a year of establishing the North American Free Trade Agreement, wages were cut by half in Mexico, while the cost of living rose by 80%.

In *Corpwatch*, "What is Neoliberalism?" (2) Elizabeth Martinez and Arnoldo Garcia point out that:

One of the indisputable results of Neoliberalism is that the rich are growing richer while the poor grow ever poorer.

During a conference at the British Museum on November 16 2000, Nelson Mandela declared:

> "We welcome the process of globalization. It is inescapable and irreversible. "However,"...if globalization is to create real peace and stability across the world, it must be a

process benefiting all. It must not allow the most economically and politically powerful countries to dominate and submerge the countries of the weaker and peripheral regions. It should not be allowed to drain the wealth of smaller countries towards the larger ones, or to increase inequality between richer and poorer regions."

JOBS JUSTICE EQUALITY
0% INTEREST IN OTHERS
FAIR TRADE NOT FREE TRADE
STOP GREED !
NO CHILD LABOR
WTO
GLOBAL INJUSTICE GREED + IGNORANCE
STOP EXPLOITING WORKERS
CAPITALISM IS NOT WORKING
WTO KILLS FARMERS
THE WORLD IS NOT FOR SALE
DEMOCRACY NOW
NO TO SWEATSHOPS
不要新自
由主
Les Gens AVANT L'ARGENT

Quoted in *Global Issues* in "Criticisms of Current Forms of Free Trade," (3) John M. Bunzl writes:

> "Far from some altruistic motive to see those in poor countries improve their lot and thus narrow the gap between rich and poor, globalization therefore merely serves as an efficient, low-cost method for TNCs [transnational corporations] to take advantage of low taxes, weak regulations and vulnerable labor whilst penetrating the economies of developing countries."

We could even go so far as to say that Neoliberalism is a factor in causing social disintegration. If it is taken for granted that economic dynamism should reward company shareholders and that other benefits for the workers or the rest of society are of secondary importance, then this economic dynamism can only occur at the expense of the social structure. It amounts to aggression with regard to social values, swindling the social organization. This is clearly shown in the measures imposed by capitalism. Just as during the Industrial Revolution, when farmers and small, independent craftsmen had to give up their independent means of subsistence and become working-class masses dependent on capital, today we can see the same damage being inflicted upon the social structure by the measures dictated by Neoliberalism – reduction of the role of the state, deregulation, the greatest possible freedom for businesses, the privatization of public sectors, reduction of the power of the unions, labor flexibility, precarity which puts employees at the mercy of their employers, cuts in social protection – all these elements demonstrate the economic masters' aggression towards the social structure for their own gain.

The most obvious aspect of this way of doing things is that the decisions which affect society as a whole are taken by a very small number of people, all with ulterior motives.

It is also obvious that this same mechanism has now spread over the entire planet.

In the same way as it generates workplace relationships based on heedless exploitation and competition, Neoliberalism puts a strain on the environment and the world's resources, causing further degradation. The "free-for-all" principle, a primitive, "dog-eat-dog" battle is placed at the very heart of the social contract, and cynicism becomes the moral foundation of our world. It establishes a moral deficit in our world which earlier societies did not experience to such a serious extent, and endorses the degradation of conditions for humankind on a planetary scale.

3. A Quick Glance at Developed Countries

There are hundreds of reports and studies highlighting the persistence and even the rise in significant levels of poverty in developed countries. We can get an idea of the situation by quoting just a few of them....

In the year 2000, an OECD report (1) on poverty in six developed countries (including Germany, Canada and the United States) indicated a disturbing rate of persistent poverty. Over a period of six years, poverty levels in these countries fluctuated between 12 and 40%.

The most noticeable differences between rich and poor are observed in the richest of these countries. In the United States, the top 1% of the population amasses more money that the 40% of people at the bottom end of the scale, and this inequality has been increasing constantly for 70 years.

In the United Kingdom, the 50% of people at the bottom of the scale possess only 1% of the nation's wealth. In 1976, that figure was 12%. Poverty can be said to affect half Great Britain's population if welfare benefits are not taken into account – a sorry result for a country which for centuries has endeavored to be a standard-bearer for civilization.

Could this be called progress? Is this fair distribution of wealth? Is this economic efficiency?

Here are a few accounts:

The Impact of Globalization on Urban Development.

(A description of an inner city neighborhood)

"Row upon row of empty, boarded up privately owned houses exist in neighborhoods where Local Authority tenants do not wish to live and owner-occupiers have abandoned properties that have become almost worthless. Escalating crime rates in these areas are amongst the highest in Western Europe, as are levels of hard drug dependency [...].

Inner London is now the wealthiest single region in Europe, with a per capita GDP more than double that of the European average. The capital enjoys a GDP three times higher than the poorest British regions [...]. Britain in aggregate is one of the four poorest countries in the European Union. It has the sharpest distinctions between rich and poor regions in Western Europe. Against London's rating of 222, the EU average for GDP per person is 100 [...].

Global economic competition leads to the impoverishment of the vast bulk of the population, while a small minority live in islands of fantastic prosperity... Areas in Britain's towns and cities that had the worst social and housing conditions at the turn of the last century are still, one hundred years later, the areas of greatest deprivation. Governments have come and gone, but urban rot continues to blight the lives of city inhabitants. Cities embody and reflect the social conditions and physical health of its inhabitants...If urban life and infrastructure are disfigured and social relations fractured, then it is because unemployment, poverty and inequality have been allowed to fester and breed..." (2)

"It is ironic that as the world's wealthiest nation, hunger and poverty in the United States still persist. Evidence shows that millions of families and children live in poverty and experience hunger. In 2004, 37 million Americans

> were living in poverty, in other words 12.7% of the population... (3)

The media tend to justify the existence of an invisible sub-proletariat class within in the world's richest society.

However, the sudden appearance of homeless people became noticeable at the beginning of the 1980s. "By the mid-1980s, seemingly out of nowhere, for the first time since the Great Depression, large numbers of individuals and families were living in the streets. "The homeless" is a social phenomenon usually associated with countries like Bangladesh, but has now survived as a visible urban fixture in this richest of countries." (4)

Inequalities in the distribution of wealth:

We seldom hear economists voicing concern about the exorbitant inequality in the distribution of wealth. We should thus surmise that the concentration of wealth in the hands of a small number of people is something completely normal and never to be questioned. Moral issues are entirely obscured by economics. It would seem, then, that those who speak for economic science have a very limited vision, or perhaps they are all partially blind. At the very most they offer some lame explanation, saying that wealth has a tendency to trickle down, although those at the bottom who do manage to catch the few drops that trickle down can clearly see that wealth is sucked up towards the top by the gigantic pumps of the neoliberal structure.

It can be off-putting to be force-fed with statistics, but those that follow are eloquent and could be of interest. They gather together some facts about the way in which the system distributes economic wealth. It is supposed to trickle down to the bottom, but this is not what happens.

Let's continue to take the United States as an example, as this country is the best model and the most ardent advocate of neoliberalism. With just a few strokes some clear-sighted journalists have outlined the whole picture:

At the very top, 5% of Americans possess 57% of personal wealth while the 50% of the population at the bottom of the scale possess only 2.8%. What's more, the gap has been widening constantly over recent decades. (5)

Movements for social justice are active, but America is being described as the richest of the Third World countries, and it is said to be drifting towards a society of economic apartheid. Poverty continues to grow, and inequality is reaching new heights. (6)

> "Real wages are declining; in fact, the share of the GDP that goes to wages and salaries has reached a 59-year low, while the share going to corporate profits is at a 40-year high." (7)
>
> The current reality is that the wealth is ending up in fewer and fewer hands. For the majority of U.S. households, the real story of the 1990s was not an expanding stock portfolio, but the plummeting of personal savings, stagnating wages, longer work hours, and the escalation of consumer debt. [...]
>
> An extreme example of the growth of the wealth gap is found in the wage gap between executives and workers. While the average worker's pay in 2000 was lower than in 1980, adjusting for inflation, CEO pay was 10 times higher. [...]
>
> We have not wanted to acknowledge that the American experiment may be failing; however, the rules of the economy have changed. There has been a clear power shift as corporations and large asset owners have influenced tax laws as well as trade, monetary, and labor policies to benefit investors rather than workers and consumers. (8)
>
> "About one-quarter of stockholding households owns stock worth less than $5,000 and the typical stock-owning household in the middle of the income distribution [...] owns only about $15,000 in stock. Most stock-owning households -- about 60 percent -- hold stock only indirectly, generally in tax-favored retirement accounts [...] In short, the majority of households lumped in with the investor class only have small stock holdings, mostly in retirement accounts." (9)

And for yet more proof of the social evolution that advanced countries are experiencing:

November 2006. France's Minister for Social Cohesion announces that shelter for 100,000 homeless people will be made available from November 1st to March 31st 2007 - 4,600 places more than last winter. In 2006, there were eight million people living below the poverty line in that country. Progress is certainly making progress!

January 2008: We learn that the employees of large investment banks (the 'Golden Boys') are to receive tens of millions of dollars each in end-of-year bonuses, even when their activities are responsible for a great number of job losses in the companies they manipulate. There is, however, an improvement on last year – firstly, the bonuses are significantly increasing, and also, there has been no report of the staff who clean their offices having to go on strike to get a pay rise, as was the case in London last year. But there is some cosmic humor – those traders have since been caught out by the crash, and they too are finding themselves on the street, at least for some time.

4. A United World for Better or for Worse

It is clear that our economic order is not keeping its promises, and is proving incapable of establishing a fair and prosperous society in developed countries, where such a society should already have existed for a long time. On the contrary – we have just seen how poverty is becoming more widespread and we are still a long way from a harmonious state of affairs.

It's true that the researchers hired by investing bodies trumpet astonishing results – we thus learn (on condition that we choose the right study methods) that thanks to globalization, poverty has been spectacularly reduced since 1980 and that on a global level, income gaps are at their lowest since 1910. Poor people living in poor countries have been the main beneficiaries of this. (1)

At the World Summit for Sustainable Development in Johannesburg in 2002, a significant reduction in poverty was noted, especially in East Asia.

The level of poverty in this region had fallen from 28% to 15% in eight years thanks to remarkable growth in countries such as China, India and Vietnam. Millions of people had been lifted out of conditions of extreme poverty.

However, this does not guarantee these people a radiant future in a prosperous, fair and balanced society, for this does not exist anywhere in the world, and will certainly not arise through neoliberalism.

In fact, if we observe all the developed countries as a whole, we can see that wherever they are in the world, they are equally distributed over the poverty scale without any distinction whatsoever.

A study has classified the countries in the following order:

> "The Scandinavian countries, plus Finland and Taiwan, all cluster at the top of the ranking, having the lowest levels of poverty. The continental European countries such as Germany, France and the Netherlands, are in the middle, while the Anglo-Saxon and North American countries have the highest rates of poverty."(2)

In other words what the future holds in store for us is not harmonious development which is satisfactory for everyone, but the long-term establishment of the inequality we are already seeing.

Mila Kahlon's article describing Mumbai (Bombay,) which was quoted in the opening chapter, continues as follows:

> "[It is] without doubt the wealthiest [city] in India. More than half of India's income tax is paid here. It is also India's most corrupt city: more than half of the black money in circulation is generated here. It has more millionaires than the other metropolitan cities put together. It hosts 90% of India's merchant banking transactions and has two stock exchange towers; 80% of India's mutual funds are registered here, where the capital markets are located [...]
>
> Real estate means money - property is more expensive than in New York and Tokyo (a posh apartment could cost up to $2m). This city indulges in speculations, lotteries, horse races and cricket. Advertising hotshots are better paid than doctors, as Mumbaikars shame the consumer society of the United States. The city attracts the best skill pool in India, multinational giants, investors, artists and intellectuals. [...]
>
> In this city you can buy French champagne for only three times the average middle-class salary, but millions cannot get a drink of clean water. Dharavi is the biggest slum in Asia, where 600,000 people are squeezed into less than two square kilometres, its air thick and sticky with the smell of human waste. [...]" (3)

This illustration reveals much about the general state of the world as a whole - a situation in which the same universal pattern appears, to a more or less extreme degree, which globalization has established everywhere, with an extremely wealthy minority possessing all the rights and all the advantages, then the middle classes, who strive to maintain the modest prosperity that the labor of their forefathers has left them with, in circumstances of great effort, uncertainty and stress, which does not make for an ideal existence – and finally, in every country in the world, the laboring classes struggling to survive in difficult conditions which are, at times, getting even worse, and which are never going to disappear.

5. The Law of the Market

The law of the market is the sacrosanct principle governing the world.

This principle has met with universal success, to the extent where it is being compared with a religion - a stunningly successful system of values (1). It might even be compared with the most extreme aspects of blind faith, and can be seen as some kind of fundamentalism. (2)

Here is a more conventional explanation:

> "In every market transaction someone voluntarily gives something to someone in exchange for something else, and expects to be better off as a result. Value is created, and each party to the exchange captures some of that value – or else the exchange would not take place at all. In other words, a market system involves cooperation for mutual benefit [...]
>
> Economics consists of analysing exactly how and why voluntary exchange of goods and services within a sound legal framework will spread wealth throughout society. The discipline of economics explores how the price mechanism signals consumer preferences and resource scarcities. It explains how the profit motive induces businesses to discover consumer preferences and cater for them at least cost. The search for profits motivates the development of new technologies and the willingness to undertake the investments likely to provide the greatest pay-back to society.

> Competition between firms to serve the consumer drives down prices and spurs innovation". (3)

Those are the ideal conditions of how the market operates, but in reality, things are not so rosy. The market is not a fundamentally just mechanism – it relies on a relationship based on power and is often far from fair. The following observations by John Ikerd, professor at the University of Missouri, highlight the system's basic flaws.

> "Economics assumes that trade always takes place between two people or groups that are equally competent and capable of pursuing their own self-interest. Sometimes this is a valid assumption, but often it is not. Economics ignores the fact that the world is filled with people (and countries) who are inherently unequal in competence and capabilities. It ignores the fact that giant corporations are capable of totally dominating conditions of trade with smaller businesses or individuals. [...]
>
> Any trade that is legal is generally accepted as free trade by economists. Economics ignores the fact that the strong may pressure the weak into trading by simply threatening or withholding benefits, or protection from harm, upon which the weak has become dependent. Since the strong are not legally required to provide these benefits, no law is broken.
>
> When trade occurs between the strong and the weak, particularly when motivated by profit as economists assume, the weak are invariably exploited by the strong. As long as the outcomes for strong and weak added together end up in a larger dollar and cent total, economics concludes that there have been gains from trade -- no matter that the weak are now even relatively weaker and more vulnerable and the strong are now even stronger and more dominant. To the economist, justice and equity are

just empty words because they have no means to address them.” (4)

The Market is, then, profoundly ambivalent. It effectively relies on some kind of cooperation, and certainly distributes resources, but at the same time it sets the participants’ interests against one another and encourages anti-social tendencies.

As Adam Smith emphasized in his work *The Theory of Moral Sentiments*, the Market is a dangerous system because it corrodes shared community values - the very values it needs to restrain its excesses. This is still the case; the values of justice and equity continue to clash with those of self-interest.

The Market is neither a law nor a principle – it is an event that occurs. It is a mechanism that may be just or unjust depending on the situation. It is in no way a fundamental and founding principle. It is a good system to manage trade and a good way to regulate exchanges, but it is by no means an incontrovertible law.

There are always at least three parties in an exchange – the seller, the buyer and the person who is left out. The exchange can only be fair when the two parties involved are satisfied and the excluded party does not express any interest in the matter. .

This means that the exchange is often unjust, and is therefore only a circumstantial event in the sharing and distribution of wealth; it cannot be the sole principle, and inevitably involves corrective adjustments. Any observer who is sufficiently perceptive and aware can see that the Market is a mechanism which systematically and unavoidably fosters inequality.

When all is said and done, it is the very mechanism of the Market that generates inequality, with wealth on the one side and scarcity on the other; by keeping as much as possible for oneself and giving as little as possible in exchange; by paying the lowest wages possible and keeping as much of the profit as one can. All the inequality that exists in our world stems from the dictates of the Market. The Market is a mechanism which breeds inequality whenever it can. That is not its goal, but it is a consequence that lies hidden in our basic lack of awareness, and whose long-term effects unbalance human society.

6. The Quest for the Highest Profit

Our basic fears, needs, desires and existential emotions are the driving forces behind the economy. The desire to survive - and to survive well – is a gut instinct.

Recognizing the principle of profit is, therefore, completely natural and justified. Comfortable prosperity is a legitimate goal, and achieving it is desirable for all of us. We all want to make sure our families have everything they need and to provide them with a financially comfortable existence so that they can then fulfill their potential in other aspects of their lives.

If the law of the market is continuously creating inequality and disparity in income, if it generates both fulfillment on one hand and dissatisfaction on the other, the cause of this fundamental imbalance lies in excessive profits.

The world of business has an attractive façade. Businessmen can be proud of their moral principles, and quite rightly so. For them, their profits are the fruit of intense and noble labor. Business relationships are founded on an irreproachable morality, and they even contribute to developing this morality. This is all perfectly true and valid, but concerns only the part of the activity which is visible and discernible. This is not the sole ethical issue at stake in business. The main ethical issue in business lies in the part that we do not see.

One does not have to look far to find all kinds of claims from businessmen and economists who see maximum profit as the supreme good, the driving force for activity and the creator of universal benefits.

For Griffiths, “the business of business is business, in which a moral standard has no relevance.” Milton Friedman makes the classic argument, “The social responsibility of business is to increase its profits.”

In his book, *Capitalism and Freedom*, Friedman argues that “there is one and only one social responsibility of business—to use its resources and engage in activities designed to increase its profits so long as it stays within the rules of the game, which is to say, engages in open and free competition without deception or fraud.”

These wise words shroud the problem of excessive profits in a veil of decency, because, obviously, they are, for the main part, amassed within a perfectly legal structure framework.

In *The Wealth of Nations*, (Book I), Adam Smith wrote:

> “Our merchants and master-manufacturers complain much of the bad effects of high wages in raising the price, and thereby lessening the sale of their good both at home and abroad. They say nothing concerning the bad effects of high profits. They are silent with regard to the pernicious effects of their own gains”.
>
> He continues:
>
> “The interest of the dealers, however, in any particular branch of trade or manufactures, is always in some respects different from, and even opposite to, that of the public. To widen the market and to narrow the competition, is always the interest of the dealers. To widen the market may frequently be agreeable enough to the interest of the public; but to narrow the competition must always be against it, and can serve only to enable the dealers, by raising their profits above what they naturally would be, to levy, for their own benefit, an absurd tax upon the rest of their fellow-citizens. [...] It comes from an order of men whose

> interest is never exactly the same with that of the public, who have generally an interest to deceive and even to oppress the public..."

It is becoming clear that the pursuit of the highest profit, currently taken for granted, represents a moral degradation of economic activity. In fact, this principle changes the nature of economic activity and perverts it. The nature of economic activity consists of responding to needs – our own need to earn a living and build up family assets as well as responding to the needs of others by providing goods and services. As soon as the main goal is no longer to meet needs but instead to amass wealth, economic activity finds itself veering off-course.

Anthropologists and historians have explained that the sense of self-interest as distinct from the collective interest did not exist in so-called 'primitive' societies; even in Europe up until the 18th century, communal moral values took precedence over individual radicalization.

> "Although we tend to view the profit motive as universal and rational [...] anthropologists have discovered that it is not traditional to traditional societies. Insofar as it is found among them it tends to play a very circumscribed role, viewed warily because of its tendency to disrupt social relations. Most pre-modern societies make no clear distinction between the economic sphere and the social sphere, subsuming economic roles into more general social relationships. Pre-capitalist man "does not act so as to safeguard his individual interest in the possession of material goods; he acts so as to safeguard his social standing, his social claims, and his social assets. He values material goods only in so far as they serve this end." (1)

In his remarkable work on the evolution of today's world, (2) Fritjof Capra has also observed that from the 17th century onwards, the old values which prevailed in the Middle Ages were gradually eroded. They stood for moral restrictions on money lending, personal gain and hoarding, and prices were required to be "fair". Trade was justified above all in order to maintain communities' autonomy. Most early societies, he points out, had no notion of the motivation of personal gain, economic profit or interest.

As we entered the modern era, society's values gradually altered. The advent of the industrial age saw the beginning of the mechanization of labor, and the first consequence was the generation of previously unimaginable profits. All the social standards changed, and gave rise to the values of our modern world. The aim of business became first and foremost to make a profit. Passion for money became the primordial value.

This socially formalized deviance is now a moral institution, because, for individuals, it is a way of "fulfilling one's potential". We get caught up in the game, we feel ourselves to be better than others, we justify ourselves by thinking that what we do is useful for society. But in reality, it is an imperfect self-realization, an inflation of the ego which feeds off the feeling of power that money gives. "We have succeeded" - we have become little lords; or a very big lord, who has put all his energy and his life's ambition into becoming the master of great wealth, as if believing that those riches will bring eternal life!

By acting in this way, we violate the fundamental principle which ought to govern all human activity – the principle of moral balance, according to which we would be content with an adequate profit.

Yet nature herself shows us the right path. Each human activity comes with some additional benefits. Is it necessary to eat? Yes, but it is an activity which also has the benefit of being pleasurable as well as necessary. Obviously, the same goes for procreation, or a good, refreshing sleep, or exercise. Every natural activity brings a sense of satisfaction. Working to earn one's living should therefore also bring satisfaction with the gratification of the job and the pleasure of making a profit.

However, this same natural principle also teaches moderation with regard to profit. We don't eat in order to bust a gut. The pleasure of a good night's sleep also determines its limits. The pleasure rewarding a virtuous act is sufficient in itself and at the same time expresses a limit. Nature shows us the way to find a balance.

Nevertheless, pleasure also has its pitfalls. If we take it beyond its natural limit, it becomes a perversion. Who knows no limits to their desires? Only deviants who pursue ever greater pleasure and in so doing discover that their pleasure becomes insatiable - slavery which fetters and degrades their natural being. It is like an alcoholic who no longer knows he is drinking too much, who cannot stop and lets himself be dragged down by the passion holding him in its thrall. In reality, the pursuit of pure satisfaction can never be satiated. Desire is, by its very nature, insatiable.

We have evolved in the wrong direction. This evolution shows us for what we are, as it expresses a way of being which is self-centered. In acting in this way, we take our self-interest to be the sole and unique code of conduct. As for the rest – it's very simple – we cannot see anything else. This exclusive egocentrism is part of our nature; it is the principle of survival. If we remain fixated upon our own profit without limitations, however, it becomes a form of addiction, just like any other biological excess, alcohol or drug abuse or perversion. It creates a mental condition where one is no longer concerned with the rest of the world or other people, but simply oneself in an exclusive way, ready to let everything fall to pieces for the sake of intimate self-gratification.

The root of all economic ills lies in the expression of this blind force which inevitably also leads to maximum exploitation and maximum consumption, as well as to the destructive ideal of endless growth. Admittedly, it is a legitimate and fundamental force, but it is a brutal, degrading force if left to run wild.

> "In the struggle to feed their blind and endless desires, people do not clearly perceive what is of true benefit and what is harmful in life. They do not know what leads to true well-being and what leads away from it. With minds blinded by ignorance, people can only strive to feed their desires....
>
> [...]As they struggle against each other and the world around them to fulfill their selfish desires, human beings live in conflict with themselves, with their societies and with the natural environment." (3)

The subjective values within us give rise to what we observe in external, objective reality. It is they that shape our society.

The problems which give us cause for complaint have their roots in ourselves, above all in the fact that we are relatively primitive creatures, overly dependent on a vision centered on our own self-interest.

A long time ago, Confucius observed "Where there is justice, there is no poverty."

Greed is glorified by those that profit from it, but it is, in reality, one of the main causes of social suffering. The pursuit of profit leads to all kinds of excess, both visible and invisible, and it is responsible for the main problems of our world. Under-development, poverty, the decline of moral values in a consumer society, ecological degradation on a planetary scale – all these things originate from a vision of human activity founded on the principle of narrow-minded self-interest.

It is a natural principle, but one which becomes a blind passion or even a powerful drug when the balance is tipped.

7. Dinosaurs

With regard to the matter in hand, we cannot help but see that for the last three centuries, the system has constantly cheated one of the trading parties. If we contemplate the world and its statistics, we can see that the most impoverished people are lacking what they have lost in trade – in other words, the excess taken from them. The freedom to do business also gives people the freedom to exploit others...

Should trading partners be portrayed as carnivores fighting over a carcass, pushing competition to its very limits in order to grab as much meat as possible, like lions or hyenas fighting over their prey? We care little about our neighbors and do not hesitate to binge as much as we can.

Is this a slightly exaggerated image? None of the images portraying the problems of the Third World and our own world is exaggerated – sadly, this is the simple, visible reality.

When we observe the behavior of multinational corporations, we often compare them with modern-day dinosaurs, roaming all over the planet and devouring everything they see around them, crushing anything that gets in the way of their primitive animal appetite. What, exactly, can they be blamed for?

They can be blamed for doing whatever they please. The facts and figures in this chapter mostly come from the website *Global Issues*. (1)

Firstly, this is due to their size and their power. We know that among the 100 largest economies in the world, 51 are multinational corporations and 49 are states. A good example is that the annual revenue of Motorola is said to be equal to that of Nigeria.

> "Today, giant corporations dominate almost every sector of local and global economies. Through mergers, joint ventures, and strategic alliances, corporations have formed "virtual" monopolies – irresponsible entities that maximize profits "upon every occasion." Corporate profits today are far larger than any concept of "normal" profit envisioned in classical economics. Corporations are inherently non-human entities – regardless of what the Supreme Court has said and regardless of the nature of their managers and stockholders. Corporations have no heart, they have no soul," writes John Ikerd in *Rethinking the Economics of Self-Interests*. (2)

Other people investigating the matter, such as Fritjof Capra, have made the same observation:

> "The nature of large corporations is profoundly inhuman. Competition, coercion, and exploitation are essential aspects of their activities, all motivated by the desire for indefinite expansion. Continuing growth is built into the corporate structure. [...] The maximizing of profits becomes the ultimate goal, to the exclusion of all other considerations. Corporate executives have to leave their humaneness behind when they attend their board meetings. They are not expected to show any feelings, nor to express any regrets..." (3)

Therefore, it is hardly surprising that they can shape the entire economic environment. In fact, they seem to shape the entire face of the planet. The unbridled capitalism of modern neoliberalism reigns over our world.

Corporations directly influence our lifestyles, encouraging a model based upon consumption. Advertising teaches people to believe that the main goal in life is to consume.

Corporations also influence the way in which the media presents things; either they own the media directly, or they support them through advertising. They have direct control over the ideas people have.

Corporations influence governments through lobbying, pressure groups and campaign contributions.

They can also influence governments by threatening to delocalize to more profitable places. At the same time, they also know how to benefit from tax advantages to set up in a country, or benefit from handouts if they are in danger of bankruptcy.

They are also, on the other hand, experts in the art of tax avoidance. They practise "transfer pricing" across borders by setting up paper subsidiaries in off-shore tax havens, and so avoid paying any significant taxes. According to Oxfam, using tax havens deprives developing countries of 50 billion dollars a year. (4)

The most polluting companies know how to throw their weight around when environmental treaties such as the Kyoto Protocol are negotiated.

They also often make the fundamental choice to manufacture goods which are not made to last and need to be replaced constantly, thus continuing to generate profits, even though this clearly goes against notions of sustainable development and saving resources.

Multinationals manage to influence international organizations such as the World Trade Organization. They know how to ensure that the rules of the game are in their best interests, both on an international level and in the countries in which they are going to establish themselves.

So these are the modern-day dinosaurs which binge upon our planet.

One would have to tug extremely hard to tear a leg of lamb from the mouth of a dinosaur – it's practically impossible, and the consequences of this excessive bingeing can only be fully understood when we look at the sorry state of the world. The ravages caused by their greed are not only visible in poor countries; they can be seen all over the planet. Inequalities, disparities, injustice and the human catastrophes that unbalanced profit create can be seen everywhere.

> “Massive "downsizing" and a shift to part-time workers demonstrate diminishing corporate concern for employees,

> while at the top astronomical salary increases (with lucrative stock options), and other unsavory practices such as management buy-outs, reveal that the executives entrusted with managing corporations are becoming more adept at exploiting or cannibalizing them for their own personal benefit. Between 1980 and 1993 Fortune 500 firms increased their assets 2.3 times but shed 4.4 million jobs, while C.E.O. compensation increased more than sixfold, so that the average C.E.O. of a large corporation now receives a compensation package of more than $3.7 million a year." (5)

This concerns large corporations, but it is fairly obvious that every entrepreneur or storekeeper, big, small or medium-sized, will act according to the same principles of exclusive self-interest. The more we think about it, the more obvious it appears that if the world displays such inequality and need, it is because our moral consciousness has not sufficiently evolved. We can justify the current state of affairs, especially if it is to our advantage. But we can also try to extend our consciousness to encompass a wider field, and try to see the situation as a whole, in an impartial way. We can then understand that even if we are wearing a handsome suit and an elegant tie, the level of our moral perception is not so different from that of predators fighting over prey or gluttonous dinosaurs, and that we act according to a principle of exclusive and limitless greed.

And yet it is extremely rare for animals to behave with no sense of balance. Predators content themselves with killing in order to eat, and do not continue their carnage indefinitely. In the same way, as animals do not drink alcohol, they are not subject to the same deviances as we are. It follows that the pursuit of excessive greed is a deviance and not part of normal behavior. We are proud to be the masters of the universe, but the manner in which we have become so is something of a failure. We have done it blindly, heedlessly satisfying our personal desires.

Such is the story of our world and its disease.

It is time for us to realize that although we see ourselves as highly evolved beings, in fact, we are not. Our moral awareness needs to evolve. What is the connection between mental awareness and moral conscience? It is but one and the same thing.

We could claim that our behavior is Nature's way, as Nature is organized so that one half of creation feeds upon the other half. Once digestion is finished, Nature returns to a state of perfect unity and perfect harmony. But this is only true to a certain extent, and we ought to try and go beyond this as it is in our conscious nature to do better. Making competition the norm for economic relations between human beings implies living according to the law of the jungle. We want to make a profit, a considerable one – a fast buck - and we grab it as best we can, and in doing so, we devour a part of our partners' existence. Who said that cannibalism was over? We blithely rob each other as we ourselves have been robbed.

But does that not mean that we are heading towards our own extinction?

8. The Growth of the Masses

The Industrial Revolution - the visible face of capitalist culture's expansion - and the distinctive social structure it produced occurred at the same time as another phenomenon – an extraordinary explosion of the human population.

To have an idea of the teeming, proliferating masses who did their best to survive in the most abject poverty, one only has to think back to the exodus of the peasant families (who, until that time had been living self-sufficiently) from the countryside into the sprawling cities the industrial age had spawned - or reread the social novels from that period. Today, the same scenario is unfolding in the big cities of the Third World. It is the same phenomenon, the same development mode - amassing wealth in the hands of a small minority while generating poverty for the masses.

One only has to visit the luxurious manor houses the large industrialists had built for themselves, modeled on the palatial mansions of bygone years. Rhode Island has plenty of such ostentatious homes, but they can be found in many other parts of the US and Europe too.

It is true that the middle classes gradually emerged from poverty thanks to the sacrifices made by their forefathers, and it's true that the middle classes are numerous and not in need, but nonetheless, they are plagued by the tensions and incertitude inherent in the social context. Their existence is far from ideal, even if their shopping carts are filled to the brim.

It seems that our economic system will never establish a balanced society, but will simply prop up a society based on inequality indefinitely; in other words, affluence and luxury for a few, and struggle, tension, poverty and insecurity for the many others.

Industrialization created the wretched urban masses, and now globalization is recreating the phenomenon in exactly the same way by destroying the values on which society used to be based. Peasant families who were once self-sufficient can no longer live off their own resources, so, looking for a way to make a living, they pour into the Third World's overflowing cities.

There is a direct link between poverty and the growth of the masses. Poor people see a large family as a better chance to get by. They have many children - far too many - because they have to. It provides the opportunity to have more wage earners in the family as well as some guarantee for their old age. A large family means security. Above all, it's an instinctive defense reaction when faced with a destiny they can no longer control.

The economic conditions which create poverty, then, are also the source of the appalling demographic imbalance rampaging across the world.

Poverty generates population growth, but the reverse is also true - we know for sure that the best way to curb demographic growth is to raise the standard of living.

A recent television programme showed a group of Indians of all ages, rummaging through a huge garbage dump, trying to find something to help them survive. An emaciated man with a long beard was asked if he didn't think it would have been better to have had fewer children. "Oh, no!" he replied, "The more of us there are, the stronger we are."

People the world over do not suspect that the volume of the human masses is a godsend for the masters of the economic system. The bigger that resource is, the easier it is to exploit. It has been the driving force behind globalization. We are unaware that our excessive numbers are working against our own interests.

If labor is a commodity and subject to market fluctuations, it is in our best interests to control the conditions of the market. The scarcer labor is, the better it's paid.

It's a pretty tragic fact that by seeking to protect themselves and improve their lot, the under-privileged are getting themselves, on the contrary, into a predicament which becomes more and more difficult to get out of. They act through ignorance and worsen their lot. In striving to ward off wretchedness by having larger families, they are merely making their plight all the worse.

The human masses are growing through inertia, from their own weight, but it is a change they unwittingly endure rather than a judicious, enlightened choice.

Human beings have a natural tendency to proliferate endlessly, like all other biological species, and so their offspring either flourishes or becomes a source of food for other species. But should we stay on that level or should we move up to a human level, one that is more aware, more responsible and wiser?

If we were just ordinary animals, our existence would be more harmonious, and there would not be disproportionate growth – our species would be regulated by the environment like any other species. But it turns out that we have exceeded animal limitations, and this is where we should intervene with responsible and sustainable development. We will have to draw upon other, essentially intellectual and moral faculties.

This has yet to happen. Here's a little joke to lighten the tone: it's lucky men are mortal, otherwise imagine how they'd end up forming a mass which would cover the whole world, piling up to form mountains, making the planet lose its balance and rocking the Earth's poles! They'd even break away and get lost in space like clouds of fish eggs!

If we think about humankind's destiny, we can see that we have not given ourselves the means to live out our destiny in harmony. As long as we cannot guarantee security and plenty for everybody, we're just not up to it. Nature is abundant and generous, and we have turned our world into a place of need, deprivation and confrontation. Nature is pure and magnificent, and we have turned the Earth into something stinking and unhealthy. We have the ability to do better, but we have not yet developed it.

We are not spontaneously developing our supra-animal moral sense, so what lies in store for us is that this moral sense will have to be developed through experience. We can only learn what we have done wrong by painful trial and error. Ecological warnings are among the most urgent signals encouraging us to develop our moral responsibility.

We believe that the evolution of the world is running its course as it should, with a few ups and downs. Because of the important positions they hold, we believe that our leaders know where they're taking the world, and that we have no choice but to trust them.

The reality is, however, that our leaders are no more evolved than we are, and they are not wise – like us, they are simply drifting along with the flow.

Those who preach in favor of demographic development are those who can exploit it in one way or another. If humanity wants to take its economic destiny in hand, this can only be achieved through collective, spontaneous awareness.

Human relationships are morally degraded by using the masses as tools of production and consumption. In reality, the masses are more than impersonal, raw material to generate cash. The masses have grown as a consequence of the system – the system itself has conjured them up. Surely they deserve better than to be treated as production-consumption objects, mere raw material kept at a convenient level of mindlessness so that they can be exploited without too much difficulty.

Mechanical diggers have replaced hundreds of workers using picks and shovels. Production line robots have taken over from hundreds of factory workers, and computers can do away with almost every office job; we are surrounded by intractable pockets of unemployment. Those who encourage demographic growth have their own motives – they do not do so for the benefit of the population.

At the moment, the collective conscience believes what those who control information want it to believe, in other words, that a large population is good for the economy, which means good for their own interests, without taking into account individual concerns or global needs. As a result, even if demographic growth has the effect of annihilating the quality of life, this is never brought to light. We should give those who are not yet born the chance to come into a world where life is better.

Our society is running off-course and we are heading towards a dead-end, creating a world which is more and more difficult to live in, and this can be seen in every aspect of life – environmental, demographic, economic, political and psychological. If we continue along this path, sooner or later human society will destroy itself.

9. A Cancer-like Growth

The advent of the industrial age resulted in alienating workers from their tools and cutting them off from an autonomous way of life. Now, as in the past, this situation is causing an explosive backlash in the uncontrolled growth of the human masses - a defense mechanism against living conditions over which people have no control. It is an instinctive, blind reaction for self-protection, as though through biological stimulation.

We find ourselves faced with a totally new scenario which shows that capital's exponential development is linked by cause and effect to the exponential growth of the masses. Humankind is of the same plasma, simmering in the same cauldron. The appearance of these two phenomena has created a third one – a novel concept which goes by the name of economic growth.

Large quantities of cheap labor are needed to generate markets and profit. And at the same time, activity distributes a certain amount of wealth, leads to numerous inventions, and raises living standards for most social classes. This combination of large amounts of capital and huge masses leads to overall "progress" - the notion of growth becomes the raison d'être for all the players involved.

Let's take another look at the imbalance on a global scale:

(Most of the figures in this chapter come from the website *Global Issues*).

If we examine the gap between rich and poor countries over the long term, we see that this was:

- 3 to 1 in 1820
- 11 to 1 in 1913
- 35 to 1 in 1950
- 44 to 1 in 1973
- 72 to 1 in 1992

It would be very interesting to set this increase in wealth next to increased demographics, especially in poor countries. The demographic explosion and economic growth are two poles of the same reality.

The connections which make our world one are, at times, very surprising when they become noticeable, so let's look at the comical yet sinister fact that for the first time in human history, the number of overweight people rivals the number of underweight people. While the world's underfed population has declined slightly since 1980 to 1.1 billion, the number of overweight people has surged to 1.1 billion.

It is possible that in the long term, growth will help poor countries rise out of poverty, but this is already a cause for deep concern, as it is abundantly clear that growth comes with many damaging side-effects. Without waiting for under-developed or emerging countries to consume as much as we do, which would require the resources of several planets like ours, the alarm bells concerning growth have been ringing insistently for a long time.

Let us take a look at what a few authors among the many from various backgrounds have to say:

> "... The current size of the human population has wreaked unprecedented damage on the biosphere, and is going to accelerate that damage. Millions of plant and animal

species have been driven to extinction. ... A billion people are hungry, morning, noon and night. The ozone layer is thinning, with consequences that are lethal for every living organism. The air, water, and soil across the planet have been fouled. The forests in many countries are gone or nearly gone. And the mammary glands of every mother on Earth are now infiltrated with DDT and other harmful chemicals. These essential facts -- truths that distinguish this century from any other in our history -- are all the byproduct of uncontrolled human fertility and thoughtless behavior." (1)

"But, equally important to a holistic, ecological view, it is capitalism which creates this irrationality and hastens the destruction of the environment in most of the world, and without destroying capitalism, neither green revolutions nor population control will put food in the mouths of those who cannot afford to pay for it."(2)

"Human activities are no longer ecologically benign -- if they ever really were. The pressures of growing populations and rising per capita consumption are now depleting resources of the land far faster than they can be regenerated by nature. Wastes and contaminants from human activities are being generated at rates far in excess of the capacity of the natural environment to absorb and detoxify them. Fossil fuels, the engine of twentieth-century economic development, are being depleted at rates infinitely faster than they can ever be replenished. Human population pressures are destroying other biological species, upon which the survival of humanity may be ultimately dependent. The human species is now capable of destroying almost everything that makes up the biosphere we call Earth, including humanity itself." (3)

It is time that we reconsidered the basic principles governing the Earth. This is an account by Frank Brunner in an article on-line, *"The Internal Logic of the Common Good"*:

> "Wherever life is observed, organization for the common good can also be seen, so that each element of an organism contributes to the prosperity of the others. In this way, the various organs are complementary, and each benefits from the smooth functioning of the others. This organizational principle can also be seen in a biotope, where vegetation, herbivores, carnivores and carrion eaters perform complementary functions.
>
> On the face of it, each one of Creation's organisms could be organized in a specific way due to chance. It is, therefore, interesting to understand why everything in Nature is organized according to a logic of common good.
>
> If the organism's various organs, or even one of its cells, functioned in an anarchic way, instead of completing each other in a logic of common good, the organism could not live. It would be fundamentally deprived of coherence. Cancer is an example of a cell multiplying anarchically, without adhering to the logic of the common good. The cancer dies along with the organism it destroys. By going against organization for the common good, it brings about its own destruction. This principle of organization for the common good is obviously a vital one [...]
>
> This organization for the common good which coordinates the development of the biotope links the proliferation of a species to the food resources available in its environment through a logic of cause and effect. The logic of the common good has the ability to exercise automatically a regulating influence on the phenomena associated with it." (4)

There is no reason why the principles which govern life on Earth should not apply to human society. On the contrary, these are precise instructions showing us what should be an appropriate way of living and where we are making mistakes.

Thus our unlimited economic growth which inevitably becomes destructive can easily be compared with the growth of a cancerous tumor.

A malignant tumor develops when a gene to suppress proliferation is lost. In the world around us, it is easy to identify the lack of normal regulation – it is caused by our moral sense of balance and equity being swamped. Greed, rather than any moral standard, has been established as the accepted principle in society.

This is how, in society just as in biological organisms, malignant growth occurs when the surrounding safety checks which ought to prevent the error no longer function. There is no longer any regulation – quite the opposite – the harmful activity no longer encounters any restraints, and by developing, acquires new capacities to proliferate, progress and resist any form of control.

We are frantically busy constantly encouraging growth as if it could continue endlessly. We don't even bother to ask ourselves that question. So obsessed are we with our immediate self-interest that we cannot even see that this unbridled growth is harmful and dangerous. It is unbalanced because it leaves to one side some social classes whose members can barely hope to receive a few crumbs, also leaving aside some crucial services in the public sector, as well as neglecting a large portion of the world's inhabitants. What's more, this hallowed growth has a totally devastating effect on the environment.

The root of the problem lies in blinkered self-interest being allowed to overstep the limits of the common good. Let us look once again at what Brunner writes:

> "All of a sudden, the behavior of a cancerous cell no longer obeys the logic of the common good which coordinates the life of all the other cells in the body. It is as though the

> cancerous cell had "decided" to proliferate in a selfish way, without taking into account the evolution of the reality within the body. And this is where one of the most fantastic features of the logic of the common good may be observed.
>
> When an element ceases to adapt to the logic of the common good, its behavior alters in a characteristic and highly significant manner. By ceasing to adapt to the evolution of the reality, by no longer complying with the logic of the common good, the disruptive element triggers the appearance of a problem, which we will call the fundamental problem.
>
> Instead of remaining stable, this fundamental problem automatically begins to activate cascades of secondary problems, which, in turn, activate further cascades of secondary problems, and so on...The logic of cause and effect relationships means that the fundamental problem, through generating cascades of secondary problems, destroys the environment upon which it depends, destroying itself in the process." (4)

We often carry a serious disease for a long time without realizing, and when it is discovered, the condition is catastrophic.

It is difficult to deny how closely this echoes the state of our society. Let us take a moment to consider our diseased humanity, which, while bingeing on energy to maintain its frenzied growth, is at the same time dying or wasting away as if from terminal exhaustion. This bears a close resemblance to the proliferation of unhealthy cells which have lost their ability to self-regulate, multiplying endlessly until the whole organism is destroyed.

The human masses and GNP are two agents which stimulate each other and form a single, prolific growth just like millions of anarchic, unthinking cells which cannot stop multiplying and consuming energy. An ever increasing population is required to create more growth, and ever greater growth in order to meet the needs of the population; more and more markets for more and more profit, more and more wealth...and then we have to create a still larger population in order to generate a little more wealth.

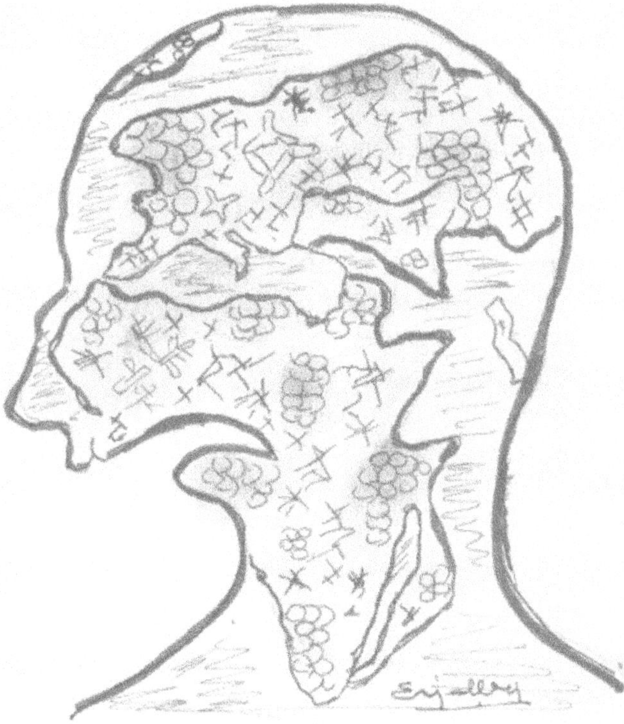

If we consider not only humankind as a single organism, but the whole planet, the image of morbid development suggests that the human population itself constitutes a form of pollution when it grows beyond its natural limits.

Some believe that a city with a population of ten million and ten thousand pizza sellers is worth far more than a city with one million inhabitants and one thousand pizza sellers, which is worth far more than a village with one thousand inhabitants and only one single pizza seller – the very image of misery, abomination and desolation, as this village has missed the progress boat. Genius is needed in business. Anyone who has a field and divides it up into twelve plots to sell for a lot of money is not a genius, as the person who buys them will divide the plots further into thirty-six plots – this person is a semi-genius in business – he will be followed by someone who will create a hundred plots – this person is the true business genius, or at least he will think so until he realizes that on each plot of land he could have built dozens of apartments, which are highly sought after. The proof is that all those who bought and then sold their apartments, making a huge profit keep congratulating themselves with their canny investment. They have not yet understood that they have not necessarily earned as much as they thought, because in order to buy another, similar property, they too will now have to pay the full price. Nothing is perfect and the road is very long for there is no end to progress.

This is a perversion, and not part of our natural code. To verify this, all we have to do is come back to the principles of Adam Smith, for whom the pursuit of self-interest contributed to producing the common good, of course, but he was well aware of the importance of moral feelings, and for him, individual profit could be nothing other than a natural, fair profit.

Determining a "fair profit" is a conscious, personal act; it is a moral act.

According to Brunner, if we observe Nature, it reveals exactly the same reasoning as Adam Smith's.

> "Even though every species – and each individual within every species - is exclusively concerned with its own self-interest, all these self-interests are interdependent and coordinated by a logic aiming to promote the common good [...]
>
> For example, if we consider the life of a tuft of grass, some elements soak up solar energy, others soak up water and others soak up nutritive elements from the soil, but each of the elements with their specialized functions participates in the prosperity of the tuft of grass as a whole. There is a general system, as though designed to coordinate self-interest within a logic of common prosperity; a logic of the common good. We can see that none of the cells which make up the tuft of grass, from the roots to the tips of each blade, is excluded from the "benefits" of this organization for the common good. This organization for the common good is, by its very nature, undiscriminating. Each of the combined cells derives a selfish profit from this common prosperity and thus, egotistically, it is in its own interest to participate in the functioning of the phenomenon. The blade of grass benefits from the activity of the root while the root benefits from the blade's activity." (4)

The rule, then, must be to find one's own self-interest within the common good, without harming it, but instead, on the contrary, in reinforcing it.

Does this mean that we are degenerates, a decadent species on the brink of extinction? Probably not; let us just say that we veer off course easily because we are not sufficiently evolved. For example, evidence shows that we do not understand this logic of the common good. The basic principle controlling our life eludes us. We see ourselves as almost perfect beings, the pride and joy of a lengthy evolution which has reached its goal in these splendid creatures, we human beings. But it does not end there. Our evolution is probably sufficient on the physical level, and satisfactory on the mental level, but it is totally insufficient on the moral level, meaning the spiritual level. We are probably only about two thirds of the way along our evolutionary road.

We think of ourselves as evolved, but in fact we do not know what we are. We are unaware of what our destiny should be, and do not know the meaning of our lives. As for making moral decisions, we are very often uncertain or wrong.

We are bathed in an immense field of intelligent energy and we cannot see it, even though we are an intrinsic part of it, and even though this intelligence which is also our own contains all the answers to all our questions.

As Frank Brunner writes in *"The Internal Logic of the Common Good"*,

> "The more we analyze this logic of the common good, the more fascinated we become by the extraordinary coherence of its conception. We see that this logic of the common good implicitly contains notions such as solidarity, fairness, freedom, etc [...]
>
> While its material manifestations are obvious for anyone who goes to the trouble of opening their eyes, the logic of the common good, however, is an invisible phenomenon which belongs to the domain of thoughts and the spirit. Its existence can be felt by logical reasoning. We can measure its effects on the material world, but we cannot measure the logic itself." (4)

We ought, then, to understand where our efforts should lie. The logic of the common good shows us the way and indicates how we should adapt to deal with our problems. We have created gigantic problems through ignorance, through a lack of awareness. Our trials and errors open our eyes. It is time to understand that our "development" and "growth" are far from really being development and growth, but are instead a form of swelling or bloating – an aberration which has become destructive.

After wasteful egocentrism, after smug ignorance, the time has come to broaden our consciousness and head towards maturity and responsibility. It is time to work at becoming people who fulfill their potential.

Let us hope that humankind has only been sowing its wild oats. We will have to stop developing only a part of our being and leaving the rest aside. It is within our consciousness that progress and growth are required. What we are most in need of is personal, subjective and moral development, and that means developing our awareness.

Realizing this is enough to set us on our way for change. Can we decently believe there is nothing to do on behalf of the children born into this world? There is a look in the eyes of a newborn baby that asks us to do well, and to do even better for those yet to come.

10. A Matter of Conscience

We have examined the world from every angle by looking at everyday, ordinary news.

All over the world, the rich classes, or rich countries, grow richer and richer, and more and more able to retain their advantages, setting them in the stone of established systems, laws and global agreements. On the other hand, poor countries and poor social classes are worse and worse off, and less and less able to change their condition and gain access to acceptable living conditions.

- The GDP of the 48 poorest nations (i.e. a quarter of all countries) is lower than the combined fortune of the three richest people on Earth.

On the one hand we have this increasing wealth, this rise in living standards, this excessive consumption, this hypertrophied stock market, and on the other, we have insecurity, destitution, hunger, disease and decay.

In fact, those who are comfortably off financially are not really well-off. Their lives are played out in frenzied traffic jams in the cities, and they are locked into rigid rhythms and structures. They are surrounded by unemployment, precariousness, material insecurity and criminality. Their lives are more or less summed up by the struggle against an ever-present, permanent malaise. Their surroundings are deteriorating and their quality of life is evaporating.

A single, invisible phenomenon is the source of this impasse – it is caused by individuals monopolizing riches which ought to be shared. The constructive reflex for personal security has become relentless and harmful. Our lack of conscious development makes us act in a way which goes against the logic for the common good and against fully understood and complete self-interest. Spiritually we are like baby moles whose eyes have not yet completely opened.

Human society's well-being, dynamic balance and harmony on every level of existence are not given to us ready-made. This demonstrates that this ideal state cannot be achieved if we give free rein to the blind impulses of self-centeredness. It also goes to show that achieving a condition of harmony and balance is our own responsibility. It is our job and our responsibility to create it, and we are free and able to do so. And, on the contrary, if we do not, nobody will do it for us. If we possessed a slightly better developed sphere of consciousness we could build ourselves a world which would astound us. We could do wonders for ourselves – this is entirely possible, but remains uncertain.

The panorama of today's world and our entire history bear witness to the horrors of which we are capable.

But we are not really aware of it. Nevertheless, we do understand that at the moment we are all putting ourselves in danger. Our human condition demands that we progress; otherwise we will hurtle towards our own downfall.

We have pinpointed the flaws which are eating away at our society, and it is all down to the immaturity of our moral consciousness. All our ills may be summed up in a behavior based on exclusive self-interest, at the expense of everything else.

Treating labor as a commodity devalues human relations. As soon as labor becomes something one can buy, man becomes a tool or instrument; he ceases to be fully considered as a conscious partner or as a person. The moral connection is severed. But labor is more than just a commodity; it is an act of creation. Labor is a person's active contribution and because of this, it entails rights more fundamental than are generally recognized.

Men from earlier times, who were more advanced morally, had enormous respect for people and the Earth. There are basic lessons for us to learn from the wisdom of so-called "primitive" people. Even today, men from prehistoric cultures may come and point out to us that we are dull-witted brutes, that we ought to be working towards becoming good and that the way ahead involves becoming better people – how can we continue to believe that morality is merely a cultural matter, and varies from country to country? There is a moral quality more profound and more universal, and essential to our being – that which enables us to recognize that someone is a good person.

Jack Hirshleifer: "Economic man is characterized by self-interested goals and rational choice of means."

His reign continues to intensify and expand, but these are fireworks marking the grand finale. His time is over. That man, deprived of moral economic values will have to relinquish his position as he is lacking the essential qualities required by human evolution.

As David Loy explains, the world's crisis is a crisis of values; a crisis of conscience:

> "The ecological catastrophe is awakening us [...] to the fact that we need a deeper source of values and meaning than market capitalism can provide [...] It is intolerable that the most important issues about human livelihood will be decided solely on the basis of profit for transnational corporations [...]
>
> More or less everybody now knows that market systems are profoundly flawed [...]
>
> We continue to reach for an end that is perpetually postponed. So our collective reaction has become the need

> for growth: the never-satisfied desire for an ever-higher "standard of living [...]
>
> The commodification that is destroying the biosphere, the value of human life, and the inheritance we should leave for future generations, also continues to destroy the local communities that maintain the moral fiber of their members. The degradation of the earth and the degradation of our own societies must both be seen as results of the same market process of commodification [...]
>
> Our humanity reduced to a source of labor and a collection of insatiable desires, as our communities disintegrate into aggregates of individuals competing to attain private ends.. . . the earth and all its creatures commodified into a pool of resources to be exploited to satisfy those desires [...]
>
> The spiritual problem with greed -- both the greed for profit and the greed to consume -- is due not only to the consequent maldistribution of worldly goods [...] or to its effect on the biosphere, but even more fundamentally because greed is based on a delusion: the delusion that happiness is to be found this way. Trying to find fulfillment through profit, or by making consumption the meaning of one's life, amounts to idolatry [...]
>
> The final irony [...] - comparisons that have been made over time and between societies detect little difference in self-reported happiness. The fact that we in the developed world are now consuming so much more does not seem to be having much effect on our level of contentment [...] (1)

We are all conscious of the reality described in this perceptive analysis. Even if we feel ourselves to be incapable of remedying the situation in any way, all of us can see that we are creating a society which is increasingly unbearable, and that the road we are taking leads to a dead end.

As Gandhi said, "The earth provides enough to satisfy every man's needs, but not every man's greed."

We are beginning to realize that if everyone consumed as much as we do in the West, it would require five or six planets like this one. That gives us a bit of a headache. We are drunkards waking up after a binge. We have consumed such a vast amount, and consumed really badly, and now we have very serious hangovers.

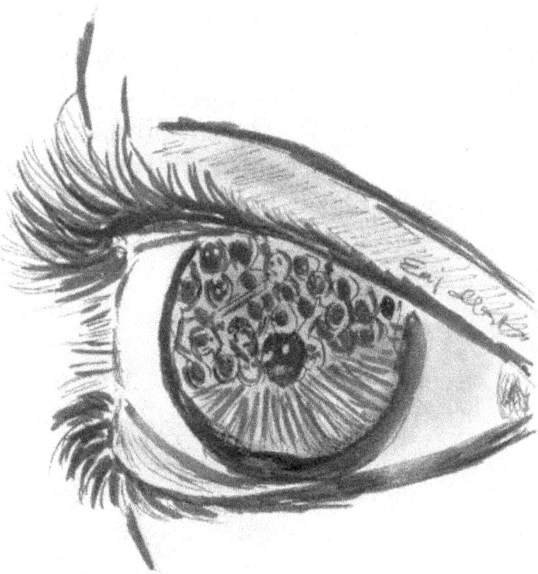

We know that the changes required mean living according to new and unswerving values. We even know what these values are.

We know that what we need to generate is not growth but quality of life.

We have developed a prodigious amount of skill and knowledge in every sphere, except with regard to a total and profound quality of life. The economic process ought to produce happiness in life. All our values need to be reconsidered. Our entire world needs to be reconstructed.

As long as we perceive of ourselves as isolated individuals in a hostile world, forced to survive by any means possible, our existence is a constant struggle and likely to grow worse. Every man for himself and against everyone else, even if one has to make pacts and form allegiances which last for varying lengths of time – this is the direction in which our world is heading on every level – personal, domestic, civic, national, international and so on, which leads to more and more pressure, more and more stress, more and more competition, false smiles and more hostility and mistrust. Taking from each other all there is to take is now the fundamental principle. This is how our world is tearing itself apart, crumbling and destroying itself over the centuries, while at the same time trying to build itself up.

As soon as we consciously perceive of ourselves not as limited and isolated entities left to our own devices, but, on the contrary, as individuals integrated into a coherent and dependable whole, everything changes. We feel ourselves to be part of a harmonious whole, not only on personal, domestic, professional, social and global levels, but also integrated on a universal level, which offers the most profound meaning. That is one for all and all for one, in natural unity. Let each give what he can - that is the basic rule to create a world of harmony and abundance. We can then feel ourselves to be part of a universe with a meaning, a meaning to which we can adhere with confidence. This other world is possible, but remains to be created.

> "The basic purpose of development is to enlarge people's choices. In principle, these choices can be infinite and can change over time. People often value achievements that do not show up [...] in income or growth figures: greater

access to knowledge, better nutrition and health services, more secure livelihoods, security against crime and physical violence, satisfying leisure hours, political and cultural freedoms and sense of participation in community activities. The objective of development is to create an enabling environment for people to enjoy long, healthy and creative lives."(Mahbub ul Haq, economist) (2)

"The restoration of balance and flexibility in our economies, technologies, and social institutions will be possible only if it goes hand in hand with a profound change of values [...] The shift to a balanced social and economic system will require a corresponding shift of values - from self-assertion and competition to cooperation and social justice, from expansion to conservation, from material acquisition to inner growth. Those who have begun to make this shift have discovered that it is not restrictive but, on the contrary, liberating and enriching. As Walter Weisskopf writes in his book *Alienation and Economics*, the crucial dimensions of scarcity in human life are not economic but existential. They are related to our needs for leisure and contemplation, peace of mind, love, community, and self-realization, which are all satisfied to much greater degrees by the new system of values."(Fritjof Capra) (3)

All in all, it remains for us to understand more fully where our wisest self-interest really lies. We know that it may well lie in the common good. As the Dalai Lama once said, whilst smiling, if you choose to be selfish, then be so in an intelligent way.

"If you think in a deeper way that you are going to be selfish, then be wisely selfish, not narrow-mindedly selfish. From that viewpoint, the key thing is the sense of universal responsibility, that is, the real source of strength, the real source of happiness. From that perspective, if in our generation we exploit every available thing, trees, water, mineral resources, or anything, without bothering about the next generation, about the future, that's our guilt, isn't it? So if we have a genuine sense of universal responsibility as the central motivation and principle, then from that direction our relations with the environment will be well balanced. Similarly with every aspect of relationships: our relations with our neighbors, our family neighbors and country neighbors, will be balanced from that direction." (4)

11. The Principles for Change

For new moral principles to be put into practice, they have to be universally accepted and experienced. For changes to take effect, they must first become part of our mentality.

Humans need to conceive of themselves in a new and different way. Limited awareness has led us to failure and to a stage in our evolution which is drawing to a close. Our new values must be both individual and universal; both inside our minds and outside of them, in everyone's minds and this would mean progress for human consciousness.

Sketching a Portrait

In Chapter 11 of his book *The Turning Point*, Fritjof Capra gives an accurate portrayal of modern, rational Man which is pretty similar to what has been called 'homo economicus':

It is, he says, the portrait of an individual who is fundamentally Cartesian, and this tends to deprive him of sound mental health. He leads an egocentric and competitive existence. He pursues his ambitions single-mindedly, and is no longer able to enjoy simple daily activities. He can only measure the quality of his life by the sum of his material possessions, and this materialism makes him concentrate on the scheming and intrigues of the external world, becoming increasingly alienated him from his inner world. In the end, he can no longer find any genuine satisfaction from this way of life. Neither fame, nor riches, nor power can fill the inner emptiness and he becomes overpowered by the feeling that his existence is irredeemably absurd, futile and devoid of meaning.

Sages sometimes speak of the blind spot we have in the middle of our retinas. For them, this represents the ego and an egocentric mode of functioning which we follow blindly, without seeing that there are things that matter beyond our personal concerns.

Pascal writes in his *Pensées*, "The nature of self-love and of this human self is to love only self and consider only self." "In a word, the Self has two qualities: it is unjust in itself since it makes itself the center of everything, it is inconvenient to others since it would enslave them, for each Self is the enemy, and would like to be the tyrant of all others".

Schopenhauer writes, "Every individual, however small, however lost, overwhelmed in the midst of a boundless world, considers himself and his own well-being before everything else, and from the natural standpoint, is ready to sacrifice everything else for this; he is ready to annihilate the world, in order to maintain his own self, that drop in the ocean, a little longer."

Sages have pointed out that our primal condition is a state of ignorance with regard to ourselves and the rest of the world. We are aware of our desires and needs and the visible world, but we miss that which is essential. This state of ignorance, life in the midst of so much that is unknown, is the sign of a consciousness which is far too limited. We see ourselves as perfect beings, the pride of evolution which has reached its term. In our heart of hearts, each of us believes ourselves to be a genius of the first order, while in reality, we are fairly primitive beings whose awareness is shallow and in much need of development. This blindness is ignorance.

We are incapable of fully understanding ourselves and of understanding our destiny and our world; incapable of comprehending the immediate and long-term consequences of our actions. This is why we live in such uncertainty and make so many mistakes on every level – personally, socially and globally. Our numerous problems stem from this ignorance. We let ourselves be driven by our basic needs and ambition. We make satisfying our basic needs the focal point of our existence, without seeing the whole picture, and without really seeing if our way of living is right, thus constantly creating strife.

Questions about Consciousness

In order to understand ourselves better, it is crucial to ask ourselves a few questions.

How does consciousness evolve? How does it grow? Many people have researched consciousness and put forward theories in which their observations echo the earliest consciousness experimenters. Some researchers have come up with original theories. One of them claims that consciousness has evolved over history and that this evolution as a whole resembles a radiant spectrum of various colors, in which each band represents a stage of consciousness. (1) (2.) Evolution has therefore undergone at least eight successive waves which blend into one another, as described in the table below:

The archaic-instinctual level (beige) in which the self can only just be distinguished from its surroundings.

The magical-animistic level (purple), seen in tribes who believe in the spirits (and modern-day gangs).

The egocentric level (red) where the self has become distinct. Seen in feudal lords, Attila the Hun, epic heroes, bandits and modern-day gang leaders. This stage includes 20% of the population.

The level of mythic order (blue). The meaning of life is part of an all-powerful order, a strict code of conduct between good and evil and in a rigid social chain-of-command. It can be found in chivalric knights, Confucius, patriotism and fundamentalism, and concerns 40% of the population.

The level of formal rationalism is orange. This involves scientific achievement, through which the self escapes the herd mentality and his quest for the truth is individualistic. Here we have an ordered world which obeys the laws of science, as seen during the Age of Enlightenment, materialism and also humanism, experienced by 30% of the population.

The color green is the level of the sensitive self. This can be seen in ecology, postmodernism, humanist psychology, human bonding, the hippy movement of the 1960s, human rights, cooperative inquiry, and pluralistic and subjective relativism, and concerns 10% of the population.

Beyond this stage, consciousness makes a quantum leap which represents a significant transformation, moving up to a second-tier which includes all the previous levels, but moves from relativism to holism and from pluralism to integralism.

The integrative level (yellow) sees the world as a kaleidoscope of natural hierarchies, systems and integrated pluralities. It represents 1% of the population.

On the holistic level of the color turquoise, 0.1% of people can see the world as a living, conscious, universal whole. This can be seen in Teilhard de Chardin's noosphere, complexity theories, and integral, holistic systems thinking.

This is one line of research among many, but what is immediately noticeable is that these eight waves of consciousness refer to the contents of evolution and not its active principle. If we look closely at the levels of consciousness described, we can see that basically, the cultural mental content changes over the historical periods. Talking about animist, egocentric or rational stages describes their contents but fails to account for consciousness itself. It lists mental content, the ideas and perceptions conveyed, the chosen focus or points of view, but it does not describe the phenomenon itself. What the phenomenon embraces is described, as well as its capacities and results - but not its nature.

There is nothing to indicate that the protagonist, the small, colorless flame setting it apart, has changed over the ages. It could probably be said that there is no difference in quality between the consciousness of a Papuan in the jungle and that of a

Nobel Prize winner. It's probably the same human spirit which has been shining continuously for hundreds of thousands of years.

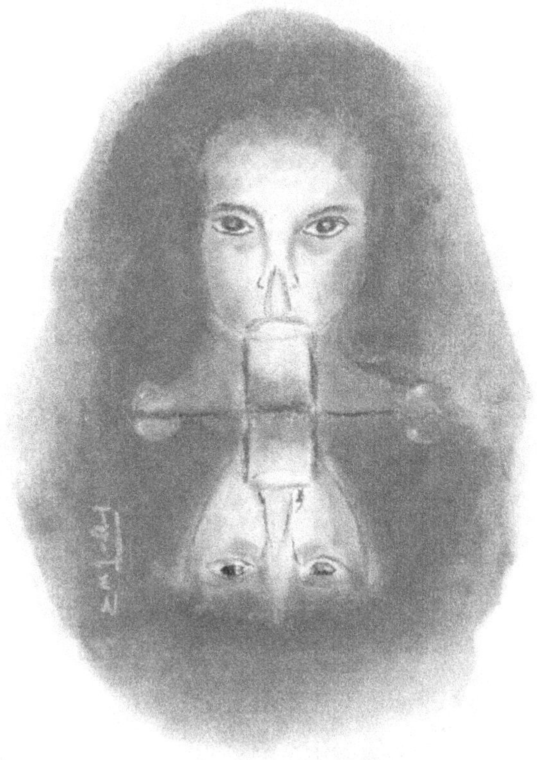

This, then, leads us to make the bizarre observation that consciousness appears to be inseparable from its contents. Content is an integral part of consciousness and consciousness is incorporated into its content. Consciousness can be compared with a mirror; we can see an image in it because light (consciousness)

enables us to see the image (the content). Without the active principle (light), there is no image, and without the reflecting surface of the mirror, there is no image either, hence the strange idea that the content of consciousness is made up of both reflected objects (material or abstract) and the light which enables it to show them, to grasp them in the mirror of the mind. This means that light and the reflected image represent one and the same truth. Consciousness and what it envisions or knows are an inextricable entity, a single phenomenon.

Internal-External Connections

What is completely clear, and totally remarkable, is that light re-emerges from the mirror. It does not vanish, but comes back, exactly as it was when it entered.

This shows perfect harmony between the external light and the mirror's inner light – it's one and the same.

If we can establish this image in our minds, we can use it as a practical tool to help us grasp the reality of human experience. Human thought can be perceived as a reflection in a mirror - the luminosity of consciousness allows us to understand things, material or abstract, through representation, enabling us to understand the world in ever greater detail and depth.

You could say that in the same way as a mirror reflects an image transmitted by light, the mind has within itself, in its reflection, information which perfectly matches that of the outside world.

The mind, as we use it in mathematical expression, faithfully reflects quantifiable information in the outside world.

Researchers claim that physical phenomena correspond to mathematical laws which can explain them, and yet these mathematical laws stem from pure intellect. The mathematical entities of the mind are in harmony with natural, external phenomena, and we find ourselves back with the mirror analogy. The light of the spirit causes an image to emerge in our minds which perfectly matches the exterior reality, just as light produces an image of the material object in the mirror.

This shows that our minds correspond perfectly with what appears to be the mind of the world. There is order, laws and organization in the universe which correspond to our comprehension. There is an intelligence in the external world which resounds in unison with our own. The content of our intellect corresponds to universal intelligence as if the field of our thought could naturally carry on outside of us, as though we were objectivising the truth of a mental field external to ourselves, one being a reflection of the other. The field may be described as a field of boundless intelligence, existing throughout the universe. It is the same intelligent energy that creates galaxies, daisies and us human beings.

How does this come to pass?

Moving from the abstract to the concrete, it's easily conceivable that the brain is the site where consciousness manifests itself. It's hooked up to the environment by sensory contacts. It works by acting and reacting with its environment, and must therefore be the spot at which primary consciousness arises, and we almost certainly share this primary consciousness with sentient animals.

This consciousness makes us aware of our existence, rooting it in time and space, here and now. It inspires the idea of a being; the self arises from it. It is a rudimentary consciousness of sensation, reaction, reflex thinking and emotions.

However, we also acknowledge having a higher level – that of reflective thought. Here, we'll have to use symbols to understand more fully. Just as a tool can be an extension of the arm, we need words to understand more fully, and use concepts which are constructed in the abstract, beyond matter, sensation or emotion. We have reached a level of consciousness which is self-aware, wondering what it is and questioning its nature and the destiny of the recently-discovered self.

We are already at the level which realizes that there is something in the universe reflecting, matching or extending our thinking.

From Individual Consciousness to Universal Intelligence

To some it may seem obvious that intelligence, or the mind, or light, already existed in the universe and that they were there before mankind appeared. It would seem that the universal mind strikes the animal consciousness of the self and is reflected as in a mirror. Or it could be said that in humans, the primary consciousness of the body takes on the role of picking up the universal mind just as a mirror picks up light. Our eyes and ears and bundles of neurons are radars which pick up and reflect external intelligence. This external intelligence then becomes both external and internal to human beings.

Even if we only feel it hazily, we may suspect that consciousness cannot merely be reduced to its physical framework.

It is hard for us to comprehend that it is not we who continually generate all our ideas. It's hard because our primary consciousness is rooted in a solid physical form, and in the self which hauls the baggage of its earlier personal experiences along with it - experiences which are more or less happy, more or less conscious, but nevertheless there, and which can cloud our understanding of ourselves.

Those who doubt that our thinking is of the same nature as universal intelligence still have plenty of time to observe the order, harmony, and beauty with which all the parts of the universe are laid out, from the largest to the very smallest. They'll see that this universal intelligence, in its sober neutrality devoid of feeling, is infinitely broader and more productive than ours, and also that ours draws strength from it like an offshoot draws strength from a tree-stump.

We are bathed in a universe of intelligent energy surrounding us, just as fish bathes in their watery world, but we are no more aware of it than a fish is aware of the water around it. Nonetheless, this intelligence is all around us, from the adaptation of the most basic cell through to the most complex organic formations (isn't it just fascinating to observe flowers?) to the movement of the celestial spheres, and this intelligence governs the universe. Yet we believe ourselves to be set apart from this intelligent environment in which we live and of which we are a part. Mind exists as much within us as around us. What could be more subjective than mathematics? The intellect determines that two plus two makes four, and this is just as true outside of us as in our conception; there is continuity between our intellect and that of the world. Beyond the consciousness of personal existence which our precious brains gather from physical perceptions, these same brains act as instruments to receive the mind surrounding them.

When a scientist in his bath jumps up shouting **"Eureka!",** it's because a new connection has been established with the universal field of the mind.

By understanding how the world works, the mind also shows us that it shapes the world. Cells are created in an intelligent manner, controlled by the mind's intelligent standards in every detail, every component and every exchange. In the same way, groups of cells form organs in an ordered rather than anarchic way. Matter manifests itself in a definite order, not random anarchy. It is the manifestation of a single energy, which spreads from its subtle, invisible source until it arrives at its concrete, tangible form.

This reminds us of the times when animist cultures felt the presence of a Spirit - let's call it an invisible force - in all beings. They recognized the spirit of the tree, the spirit of the mountain, and so on. We no longer know how to do this, because we are concentrating too hard on our own personal concerns. Although we've lost this power, however, we may one day be capable of accounting for it.

The question remains – how can we develop our consciousness in such a way as to fit in with the world's cycles better, lead a harmonious existence rich in meaning, eradicate excess suffering and error, and arrive at universal values?

Until now, we have been muddling along mostly through ignorance and with a lack of awareness.

Our minds cry out to understand better, to move on from this self-centered vision. We must surely feel this need. Our minds have urged us on to achieve fantastic success in technological inventions and research as well as artistic creation, etc. What's more, it spurs us on to seek harmony, within and outside of ourselves. The desire to do well and the desire for well-being are as fundamental as satisfying our basic needs for survival. Our consciousness clamors to see further and more clearly. The need for harmony is the very essence of our being, the basic substance of our soul.

Consciousness is partly developed through developing knowledge. Even if it does not change the nature of the perception, it at least broadens the mirror, allowing a richer, fuller representation to penetrate. It has been the human mind's quest since the beginning of time.

As soon as it identifies sensations, as soon as it generates images and concepts, consciousness applies itself in the field of thought, the infinite territory of universal intelligence which it explores and creates at the same time, in which it is the actor and the elusive driving force. It is a presence, a presence unto itself, exploring and reporting what it discovers.

From the Individual Consciousness to the Collective Consciousness

Broadening one's consciousness, then, involves developing knowledge, drawing from the field of energy in which we are bathed. At the same time, we realize that this expansion of our consciousness cannot be exclusively individual. What is attained, and what is yet to attain, is open to everyone.

Broadening one's consciousness means reducing the distance between oneself and others, moving on from an egocentric way of being and achieving a broader awareness.

Here we could quote Albert Einstein's appeal:

"A human being is a part of a whole, called by us universe, a part limited in time and space. He experiences himself, his thoughts and feelings as something separated from the rest... a kind of optical delusion of his consciousness. This delusion is a kind of prison for us, restricting us to our personal desires and to affection for a few persons nearest to us. Our task must be to free ourselves from this prison by widening our circle of compassion to embrace all living creatures and the whole of nature in its beauty."

Individual consciousness and collective consciousness are very closely bound. Collective consciousness is the exteriorization of individual consciences, a projection of individual, formulated, mental contents, an abstract grouping together of knowledge which makes up a culture.

Collective consciousness works like a generalized consensus within diverse groups, both large and small. There is a certain consensus within families, organizations, companies, clans, sects, churches, nations and cooperatives. And surely also on a global level...

A society's collective consciousness is generated by acquired knowledge. This stems from the society's experience, creating the social and cultural fabric. This is how religions, the arts, sciences and political institutions come into being.

In the society in which we live, we depend on the culture to which we belong. We are marked by it as though we'd been soaked in dye. We are conditioned by ways of thinking which are particular to each society or group, and which may be wrong. Our consciousness may be contaminated by our social and cultural environment, just as it may be contaminated by our personal experiences. We are prisoners of these bad habits and twisted thoughts and emotions, and we have no choice but to follow them. We cannot escape them. It's like when we dream, we have no choice but to go with the dream – we are not free to escape it or to change it; we just have to submit to it. In the same way, our habitual ways of thinking are a liability which dominates us and from which we cannot escape, unless we develop greater awareness.

Apart from the cultural and educational environment into which we're born, individual consciousness also broadens out towards collective consciousness via the spread of information. This objectivizes existing content and at the same time proceeds to propagate it.

Information, however, is obviously not neutral. It's often incomplete or has been manipulated. It serves those who deal it out. The media generally belong to private groups. Information is like a baby's bottle, into which one can put (or leave out) whatever one wants, in whatever doses, and it's variable, depending on who it's aimed at. However, the consequences of this are only important up to a certain extent. The most important information for the future of the human race always gets through eventually, of its own accord.

We are talking of consciousness which is individual and collective as well as universal, in other words, the extent to which an individual judges and assesses what he receives from the media. With no commentary, the facts can speak for themselves. Regardless of interpretation, all the facts paint a picture which makes sense and this sense gets through. Something remains in common to all the people of the same moral level, beyond the gaps in information, which amounts to their collective consciousness, whether or not they know each other, and whether or not they are connected in any way. They have reached the same place in the universal field of the mind, which is both in them and beyond them, and so a web of interpersonal values forms, an intellectual reality, continually evolving as the world evolves.

This collective consciousness really isn't out of our reach. It's already present within us and all around us, and seems to create itself.

Synchronicity bears witness to this. Great historical movements have always emerged from the collective consciousness. New notions do not emerge in isolation in any field of activity. Discoveries are often made around the same time in different places, sometimes very distant geographically, without those involved being in contact with each other.

We could even go as far as saying that interpersonal consciousness can have a collective effect, by spontaneously inducing changes in the social environment where it occurs; a drop in the crime rate, for example, or less interpersonal friction…

If we're sufficiently mentally alert, we might be able to see another direct link between individual consciousness and collective consciousness – in how progress made personally by isolated individuals contributes to the progress of the whole, even if this is not quantifiable. Individual and collective consciousness interact and mutually influence each other in both directions, even without verbal communication.

This may provide us with a way of doing something about the world's seemingly overwhelming problems. All those who work on improving themselves help the rest of us. What we create in ourselves through our own personal development benefits society as a whole, even without any perceptible direct communication.

An Assessment of our Collective Consciousness

This outcome is in constant evolution, and shows that remarkable progress is being made. We should congratulate ourselves! Scientific research, practical experience and general information lead to a concern for the common good which can be seen everywhere.

Everyone is concerned about environmental problems, the harmful effects of unchecked growth and so on, and everyone is ready to do his or her bit like Colibri (from the South American tale in which a fire was raging in the forest and all the animals were running away, but little Colibri, the hummingbird, wouldn't stop bringing drops of water to throw on the fire, determined to do his bit against all odds).

We arrive at universal values which are also incorporated by those involved, and are thus also individual values. New, cleaner standards have appeared throughout the world. If the world is becoming cleaner, it is because our consciousness has become cleaner and more responsible. In politically advanced, culturally liberated countries, demographic growth is wisely slowing down towards a point of healthy balance.

In any case, we are inexorably evolving from a consciousness centered on personal needs towards a broader consciousness which calls upon our maturity and responsibility. But let's not force this advanced consciousness to appear, it is coming to us by its own means, it's already here. The various quotations and facts in these pages are an example of it. At this moment in time, the collective consciousness existing in the world has all the information it needs to transform global society.

12. For the Happy Few

Even so, the collective consciousness' progress remains slow and scattered. Progress occurs in fits and starts as we gain knowledge, mostly through trial and error. The mistake has to be made before it can be corrected. It is a long, drawn-out process.

As for scientific research, it concentrates on the external world and runs the risk of not reaching the inner depths of our being, only its manifestations. It is moving away from the center.

Consequently, the results it reaps are various and overabundant, with a tendency to accumulate endlessly without coming to a final conclusion, and it may never be able to do this.

Then, progress in consciousness is made through knowledge, in other words, on the cognitive level of conceptual thinking and intellectual content. On that level, we understand and change our external actions, but this does not mean that the person's profound self is truly or rapidly transformed. There is a huge difference between what we know and what we are. It will take a very long time to arrive at values which are totally universal and individual, which allow creatures such as ourselves to progress, as we lurch from one mistake to another and from one disaster to the next

There is another way to broaden consciousness, which, rather than learning, involves developing profound knowledge, also known as wisdom.

A certain number of people are interested in this, and have already experimented with it – a small percentage of people, but, let's hope, enough to start a reaction.

This way consists of heading not towards the object, but towards the spirit, or towards oneself, the inner self, towards the center. Science stops with concepts, but this other way goes beyond that, where science cannot go, towards a perception that is unitive rather than dissociative. Instead of making intelligence work by means of ideas, it entails allowing the intuitive vision to grow. It entails developing consciousness and the spiritual level, not through reflection but outside any reflection.

It is the way of meditation or mystic integration.

It involves putting the mind in contact with itself. It is a very ancient practice seen in traditions in most parts of the world.

We can look at what tradition has to say about it.

For the Indians, the levels of consciousness described are wakefulness, sleeping and dreaming. They then observe consciousness on a transcendental level in meditation, then on a fifth, cosmic level, then a divine level and lastly on a level of final unity.

We can see that consciousness can evolve towards higher levels of perception, always in the same direction, moving away from individualism and egocentrism to see the self and the world as a single entity, a universal Self. It is a slow progression towards our own true nature, the one we do not know. It should be seen as human creatures' normal, natural path, the necessary, inevitable path of spiritual development, although it will take infinite time for everyone to reach it.

In order to develop consciousness through meditation, one has to turn towards the mind itself. Consciousness is pure spirit, present unto itself and prior to any content. You can't see it under an electron microscope or in a particle chamber. It is spirit without any other subject but itself, no object but its own presence, its own vigilance. It cannot be reduced to a concept, as it is there before concepts, sensations, emotions or feelings are formed. This original spiritual energy, the emptiness which is something within the void, is neither wave, nor particle.

Consciousness is like an imperceptible agent or invisible light. This brings to mind Kierkegaard's remark "The supreme paradox of all thought is the attempt to discover something that thought cannot think."

Development which occurs through meditation is, therefore, beyond any concept or image, in vacuity. This vacuity is not nothingness, it is a state of emptiness which contains "that which has not yet been created", meaning what has not manifested itself. The spirit comes into contact with its elusive origin which is its own essence. Here, doing nothing and perceiving nothing, by acting without acting, consciousness is silently enhanced.

Obviously, this is no mean feat. One should expect nothing and demand nothing, for what happens does so regardless of any personal resolve. One doesn't necessarily notice any progress straight away. It is a long, drawn-out process requiring a lot of patience, which should preferably be learnt from teachers steeped in tradition and experience.

By going back to the practices of an ancient tradition, we can avoid falling into the hands of the gurus, great and small, who lead sects. Recent teaching has nothing new to offer and sometimes relies on delusions or dubious fantasies. The ancient teachings are substantial enough to break a camel's back, but it's possible just to take note of the practical parts or, if necessary, just the answers one needs.

Relaxation methods adapted from ancient traditions, such as sophrology, represent an important first step and provide a useful practical approach.

A great number of meditation techniques exist. One of them consists of approaching it as a work of cleansing or decontamination which enables us to get closer to our natural inner being. We can consistently, but in a relaxed way, empty, or rather let go of all that is in our heads - all our ideas, our expectations, our preconceptions, happy or unhappy emotions – absolutely everything, as if to reach a "zero-point of stimulation" and what remains is pure consciousness which is spontaneous and does not go wrong.

However, this should not mean alienation. One can concentrate on a central point of the body. One should stay in a state of relaxed peace, comfort and serene happiness. This is what meditators do when they establish a mental "vacuity", and a vigilant but unoccupied mind.

If we can manage to spend about twenty minutes a day practicing this exercise which consists of putting ourselves outside of any rationalization, outside of any conceptualization, letting everything we have in our minds disappear – absolutely everything with no reservation, even the very idea of what we are actually doing, then we can feel our consciousness being liberated and our spirit being rejuvenated and revitalized in the mental field of original intelligence.

Over time, we can feel ourselves changing little by little and becoming happier, lighter, and more tolerant; we have a wider, improved understanding; we may even find ourselves understanding new perspectives which had never occurred to us before and want to continue along this path towards renewal. Real evolution occurs, evolution which becomes perceptible and useful instead of being uncertain, limited and diluted over the duration of our lives. We acquire wisdom, which means a better understanding of ourselves and the universe.

Over the long term, the consistent and prolonged practice of meditation leads us to attain subtle consciousness and radiance of the spirit. This is the source of the thoughts which allow us to understand external phenomena, but here, in this exercise, it comprehends itself, in a non-dual mode. We touch upon the source of our spirit and the profound nature of our beings.

This increased depth changes the state of consciousness. It goes beyond the level of reflective thinking, which always relates to subject-object, the ego and the world. A change occurs, a quantum leap, as they say, which is called the phenomenon of enlightenment. Consciousness regains its completeness, becoming cosmic consciousness, seeing itself as one with the universe. It moves beyond the narrowness of the ego and the limitations of duality for once and for all. When meditators reach cosmic consciousness in this way, they reach enlightenment of the individual consciousness which can finally comprehend the vision of the universe as a whole. The individual then sees himself incorporated into this huge field of universal spiritual energy. He is freed from any worries, grasping the integration and permanence of his being and reaching profound, serene and constant happiness at the same time as he is rid of all the petty demands of the ego.

And there's more to come! The same phenomenon is accompanied by a profound and tranquil joy as well as a spontaneous opening up to universal compassion, which clearly shows that our souls are moral in essence.

Not everyone who tries succeeds, but the door is never closed. The important thing is to follow the path, for progress will be made along the way; inner positivity will increase and the benefits it brings will keep coming. The phenomenon may even occur in people who are not expecting or looking for it. There are many accounts of this, and not only in spiritual circles.

There are also the views of many modern psychologists, similar to those of renowned scientists who understand that spirit and matter form a single entity, thus echoing the view of mystic traditions. Seeing spirit and matter as complementary expressions of a single phenomenon makes it possible to conceive of the idea of a cosmic consciousness.

Meditation should not be seen as an abnormal or artificial practice. The resulting benefits and well-being are natural reactions. During meditation, it has been observed that the brain's electrical waves alter to lower frequencies (those of relaxation, of consciousness with no external activity) while the level of endorphins temporarily increases, suggesting a rise in neuronal transmission and therefore reception.

In reality, all of us enter a state of meditation spontaneously, for example when we are working in our vegetable gardens or taking the time to knit or draw or paint a picture, or when we pause for a while in silence contemplating a beautiful landscape and then realize that we haven't noticed time passing. We have remained aware, but have lapsed into absence without realizing and have made an unexpected detour outside time. Meditation simply activates and boosts a normal process on the path to our evolution. It can be done without any religious commitment – and besides, it is strongly believed that some animals meditate.

Our hectic modern culture does not allow us to fully connect with our spiritual, energetic environment – earlier generations had far more opportunity to do so, and therefore, it's completely justified to devote oneself to meditation regularly, to benefit from this revitalization which we all need. It's a natural moment to refocus oneself, to center and gather oneself in silence.

Meditation is not just a source of well-being and understanding, it's also the way which allows us to achieve our potential and rid ourselves of our faults and limitations. It gives us the means to become better than we are and improve our fate over time.

It is a practice which helps us refine who we are, and consequently, it's an extremely positive way to deal with the problems of our existence. In his on-line book *"Buddhist Economics*" the Venerable Payutto writes:

> "Meditation helps us to see how ethical and unethical behavior are the natural consequence of the mental conditions which motivate them. Individual people, classes, races and nationalities are neither intrinsically good nor evil. It is rather our mental qualities that guide our behavior toward the ethical and the unethical. Greed, hatred and delusion drive us to unethical acts. Wisdom and a desire for true well-being guide us to ethical behavior and a good life.
>
> With meditation, we gain perspective on our motivations: we sharpen our awareness and strengthen free will. Thus, when it comes to making economic decisions, decision about our livelihood and consumption, we can better resist compulsions driven by fear, craving, and pride and choose instead a moral course that aims at true well-being. In this way, we begin to see how mental factors form the basis of all economic matters, and we realize that the development of this kind of mental discernment leads the way to true economic and human development." (1)

13. The Ways in Which Change Is Occurring

Living systems evolve of their own accord. They devise the transformations they require as the need arises. The same thing happens with global society.

A living system's evolution is activated when internal fluctuations have driven it to a state which is far from being well-balanced, reaching a critical point which demands further adaptation.

Global society has reached this critical point, and is becoming aware that it has reached a state which is not worthy of humanity. Society is waking up to the breakdown between the social strata and between various countries as well as to the collapse of our ecological surroundings. The imbalances caused by the neoliberal regime are inexorably forcing human society to adapt in new ways to try to resolve our current problems.

For over half a century, society has been stirring with movements to initiate its evolution. The social unrest and student movements in the 1960s, counter-culture movements such as the hippies, consumer groups, feminists, ecologists, anti-nuclear protesters, pacifists, human rights groups and NGOs, and, more recently, organizations for economic justice, anti-globalization and pro-fair trade are all movements which seriously call the system into question and contribute to changing it. We can add to this list all the demonstrations against wars of which people do not approve, trade union demonstrations against delocalization and political demonstrations against injustice for minorities or forms of apartheid, as well as social forums. These movements are varied and dispersed, but they are also connected by countless local and international networks. They are part of an active, established and permanent phenomenon. Through these movements global society is looking for a way to evolve. This growing awareness is shooting out in many different directions and will eventually give rise to the birth of a global society founded upon new economic and intellectual principles.

To brighten up our day, let's take a quick look at some of the most beautiful moments of this awakening:

In May 1998, 70,000 people formed a human chain around a building housing the G8 in Birmingham, England, to hand over a petition bearing 1.5 million signatures in support of the Jubilee 2000 initiative to reduce the poorest countries' debts (see the *Global Issues* website). (1)

In 1999, the human chain around the G8 building in Cologne was made up of 35,000 people who had been joined by several famous pop stars.

Also in 1999 were the notorious anti-globalization demonstrations in Seattle, which brought together hundreds of organizations from all over the world. These mass demonstrations were to protest against globalization for the benefit of big international capital at the expense of the working classes - without any open, democratic process. However, these objectives were not brought to light clearly in the media's reporting. The protests were followed by those in Washington in 2000 against the World Bank and the International Monetary Fund.

In 2000, the G8 meeting in Okinawa was surrounded by a human chain of 27,000 people protesting against militarism and third world debt.

In 2001, 100,000 people demonstrated in Genoa. A human chain in a circle is extremely eloquent. It shows solidarity, determination, fraternity, growing awareness and personal commitment.

After this, the movement for global economic justice changed gear, moving to a higher level, now not only in the streets but also on a governmental level. In Doha in 2001, emerging countries refused to bear the cost of liberal and unfair world trade. South America saw the election of left-wing governments determined to reestablish more justice with regard to the advantages that multinationals have been granting themselves. In Brazil, Venezuela, Chile, Ecuador and Bolivia, a new wind was beginning to blow, sowing ideas which continue to establish themselves and are gradually being implemented.

So let's now take a closer look at those ideas. They revolve around a particularly revolutionary notion and illustrate to what point the changes occurring in the world are fundamental. The competitive system is beginning to collapse. It has had its day. It was the battle flag of free-market capitalism and the evils that went with it, but it was a mistake.

Economists were very happy to borrow Darwin's idea that our world is a place of brutal struggle where the only fittest survive. Competition is at the heart of business; internal competition to ensure high performance and external competition to seize a share of the market. The law of the market is the law of nature and the law of the jungle, the survival of the fittest. These laws endorse predators devouring a carcass, trying to grab as much as they can for themselves (raising the impromptu question – is the world a carcass?). The marvelous theory of Social Darwinism enables business people to benefit as much as they can from their position on the one hand, and, on the other, to crush those weaker than themselves mercilessly. It was, supposedly, scientifically justified. It justified the share of power and profit in capitalism. This theory continues to shine at its zenith and current economic discourse is still advocating competition free from any kind of restriction.

But it turns out that those ideas are now completely out of date. Admittedly, competition has a role to play to maintain healthy businesses, and challenge can encourage creation and innovation. But this is not as fundamental or universal a factor as has been made out. There is, of course, competition in Nature, but it is incorporated within a more general framework of cooperation. Modern science proves that cooperation or symbiosis is the most universal principle in living systems' organization, from single-celled organisms right through to the higher forms of life. It is thanks to the partnership between several species and also within the species itself that life has been able to continue and evolve.

The essential principle with regard to maintaining and developing life is not competition but cooperation, not cannibalism but mutual assistance. As early as 1902 Kropotkin showed that the driving force behind evolution was not principally competition within a species for limited resources, but instead cooperation within the species to increase the chances of survival when faced with harsh external conditions. He claimed that when circumstances put a community (human or animal) in danger, it reacted by increasing its communal cooperation. Exactly the same thing is happening in today's world.

The competitive world is a world of struggle, antagonism, destruction and divisiveness – on an international scale between countries, intra-socially between classes, in business and in employment. It has modeled our lifestyle on a pattern of aggression and struggle resulting in our frantic way of life. It creates omnipresent and permanent stress which insinuates itself everywhere, into family life and the individual psyche. It puts individuals in a situation where profound and genuine self-realization is impossible. It is the exclusive pursuit of self-interest, but this can never be attained. It is a delusion dominating our minds like a dream that we have to live through and from which we cannot escape; a state where well-being is never really attained, even for those who are the best-off in the system. It is a life of dependency where harmonious balance is never reached. A system which consists of taking advantage of the weak necessarily requires the weak, and has to create them in order to prosper. It keeps people dependent in order to exploit them. Taking their resources from them forces them to remain dependent and the greatest dependence is still the proliferation of the masses for whom the task of development becomes practically impossible.

The competitive model is one in which we are constantly exceeding all natural limits. Everything which does not help maintain balance goes against the universe's natural order – it is harmful and a painful, unwholesome experience. We must live our lives within a harmonious system of balance, which in no way means a static balance set in stone. In order to be natural, this equilibrium should resemble that of a living organism, a dynamic balance which is constantly renewing itself, waxing and waning during exchanges, but retaining a healthy, harmonious stability.

As systems evolve, they seek their path freely; they are self-generating and invent and create the solutions they require. It is a complex process which occurs through the coordination and interdependence of various elements, incorporating them into the system on several levels, perfecting functions and modes of action. It is a progression towards more coherence and a new order.

It would be useful, then, to look at the basis from which a new order could arise. Before we do so, however, it should be made clear that these are natural, spontaneous changes which take place by themselves. Think back to the timeless quotation from the *I Ching* or *Book of Changes*:

> "After a time of decay comes the turning point. The powerful light that has been banished returns. There is movement, but it is not brought about by force... The movement is natural, arising spontaneously. For this reason the transformation of the old becomes easy. The old is discarded and the new is introduced. Both measures accord with the time; therefore no harm results."

In any case, we should realize that it is impossible to stop capitalism. It will carry on until it has run its course, in keeping with its principles. It has to continue its immoderate race towards growth without any other outcome than generating need, waste and inequality indefinitely.

This should not stop us from defining what must be the promise of a cooperative world, or which needs will become the motivations for future change. Moving from a competitive world to a cooperative one is to pass from one state to its opposite. It also means understanding that we have to reconcile opposites which appear to be inherently opposed, but which, in the end, can be harmonized, such as being able to find one's self-interest within the common good. Moving to a cooperative world also implies the following:

Moving from a logic based on profit to one based on need. Business must primarily consist in responding to a need. At the moment, business people seek, above all, to make money, and in order to do so, offer a product or service. Cooperative entrepreneurs try first and foremost to respond to a need, and any profit will be an added extra, but if there is no profit, their business will nonetheless be justified.

By heading in the opposite direction from the competitive world, the cooperative world would fulfill the promise to move from the lack of satisfaction of needs to their satisfaction, from the destruction of the biosphere to its conservation, from social disintegration to integration, from unemployment to full employment, from painful mutations to gentle transition, from insecurity to security, from aggression to fraternity, from unthinking, harmful amorality to enlightened morality, from dependence to autonomy, from dullness to creativity, from illiteracy to education, and from proliferation to responsible, social balance.

Ah, is that all?! No, it probably isn't. All this is within our reach, and we cannot yet fully imagine what humanity is capable of once it is liberated from its passive, immature lack of awareness and takes its destiny into its own hands. Not only is all this possible, but it is already well underway.

In his article *Rethinking the Economics of Self-Interests*, John Ikerd points out

> "Common sense demands that we rethink and directly challenge the fundamental principles that underlie conventional economic thinking…
>
> People will pursue their self-interest – it is an inherent aspect of being human. But, people, by nature, do not pursue only their narrow short-run individual self-interest. It is within the fundamental nature of people also to care about others and accept the responsibilities of humanity. Rethinking does not require that people deny their self-interest. Instead, it will require that we rise above the economics of greed to an economics of enlightenment. The invisible hand can still translate the pursuit of self-interests into the greatest good for society, but only if each person pursues an enlightened self-interest – a self-interest that values relationships and ethics as important dimensions of our individual well being…
>
> We can choose a life of quality -- with enough income to sustain us physically, enough friends and neighbors to sustain us socially, following a code of ethics and morality that will sustain us spiritually." (2)

In Chapter 2 of *Buddhist Economics,* the Venerable Payutto writes,

> "As they struggle against each other and the world around them to fulfill their selfish desires, human beings live in conflict with themselves, with their societies and with the natural environment. There is a conflict of interests; a life guided by ignorance is full of conflict and disharmony."
>
> *(The meaning of 'ignorance' here is very close to blindness or unawareness. Similarly, the word 'wisdom' refers to a heightened awareness.)*
>
> "When ignorance is replaced with wisdom, it is possible to distinguish between what is of true benefit and what is not. With wisdom ...we no longer see life as a conflict of interests. Instead, we strive to harmonize our own interests with those of society and nature. The conflict of interests becomes a harmony of interests. This is because we understand that, in the end, a truly beneficial life is only possible when the individual, society and the environment serve each other." (3)

14. Observing the Changes

Over the course of history, many attempts have been made to establish a more satisfactory economic system than mercantilism or capitalism, but all those which were planned and imposed by revolutions or decisions based on doctrines ended in failure. An example which springs to mind is Owen and Fourier's Utopian communities. Like the disasters caused by communism during the twentieth century, they aimed to create an ideal society, but they did so from the basis of a preliminary, abstract idea which then had to be imposed upon the external reality. Failure was predictable from the outset.

The changes which have been set in motion in today's world are different as they are taking place within society itself in a self-generating way like all adaptations of living systems. This gives us every reason to believe that we are witnessing a genuine transformation of society stemming from its growing awareness and its members seeking a new balance. Rather than being a project, it is a process which is taking place, branching out in several different directions and involving various aspects, defining itself as it goes along without its final outcome being known in advance.

Movements such as the microcredit movement in Bangladesh which began in 1976 are appearing spontaneously. It is like the natural motion of a pendulum which reaches its furthest point and then returns in the opposite direction; once a general tendency towards excess has reached its culminating point, the tide begins to turn. Microcredit has meant that the world's most dispossessed and destitute people now have the means to overcome their powerlessness and set off on their own along the path of development through self-help and solidarity. Microcredit creates networks of solidarity, kick starts various sectors of the local economy, improves women's status and people's access to social protection while gradually transforming society through its own devices.

"Once we learned that hunger results from antidemocratic political and economic structures that trap people in poverty, we realized that we couldn't end hunger for other people. Genuine freedom can only be won by people for themselves." (1)

What is true for hunger throughout the world also applies to every other need.

The microcredit movement has now spread all over the planet, wherever the needs of the poorest sectors of society have managed to set it up. Currently up to 500 million people benefit from it.

The modern renewal movement has taken on different forms elsewhere for those who have suffered the most from the injustices of our individualistic society. A characteristic of the natural, inventive evolution of living systems is that spontaneous creativity takes on various different forms depending on its needs.

During the 1980s in Latin America (where entire sections of the population were excluded, which naturally drove them to invent ways to survive), various types of solidarity-based economies sprang up and are continuing to grow.

In Brazil, the Landless Workers' Movement managed to expropriate unused land, and at least 350,000 families have benefited from it. In Argentina, factories were reclaimed and started up again by their employees so that the owners who had abandoned them were no longer able to claim them back.

Powerful networks of solidarity-based economy exist in many South American countries, and the most remarkable example of this can be found in Venezuela.

In an article entitled *"Venezuela's Cooperative Revolution"* (2), Betsy Bowman and Bob Stone report on what they have seen and heard.

Most of the people they met were connected with cooperatives. Furthermore, the State is responsible for protecting and promoting cooperatives. Under Chavez' government, they have increased in number from around 800 to more than 108,000 in 2006, and have one and a half million members. Every area of activity is involved; mutual credit companies, services, shops, restaurants, hotels, transport, communications, agriculture and, more recently, industrial production. The scale and speed of the cooperative phenomenon is unequalled anywhere else.

This is the result of a deliberate choice to turn the situation around completely in order to confront the situation head on, so that people no longer beg for crumbs, but can take charge of their own destiny, and no longer have to beg for work, but can invent their own jobs. Mission About-Face, launched in 2004 encouraged people to act for themselves using their own means to create cooperatives, thus beating unemployment and social exclusion by changing production relationships.

Autonomous development means being "capable of producing the seed that we sow, the food that we eat, the clothes that we wear, the goods and services that we need, breaking the economic, cultural and technological dependence that has halted our development, starting with ourselves." Clearly, the ideal tool to create something out of nothing in this way is not financial capital but rather human capital and cooperative organization.

It is worth noting that, just as the gap between rich and poor people exists in every country, in the same way, movements for a solidarity-based economy are appearing everywhere, even among the middle classes which are also dissatisfied with the style of the market economy. This is how various consumer, childcare and building cooperatives were born, as well as eco-villages and other similar structures all over the world.

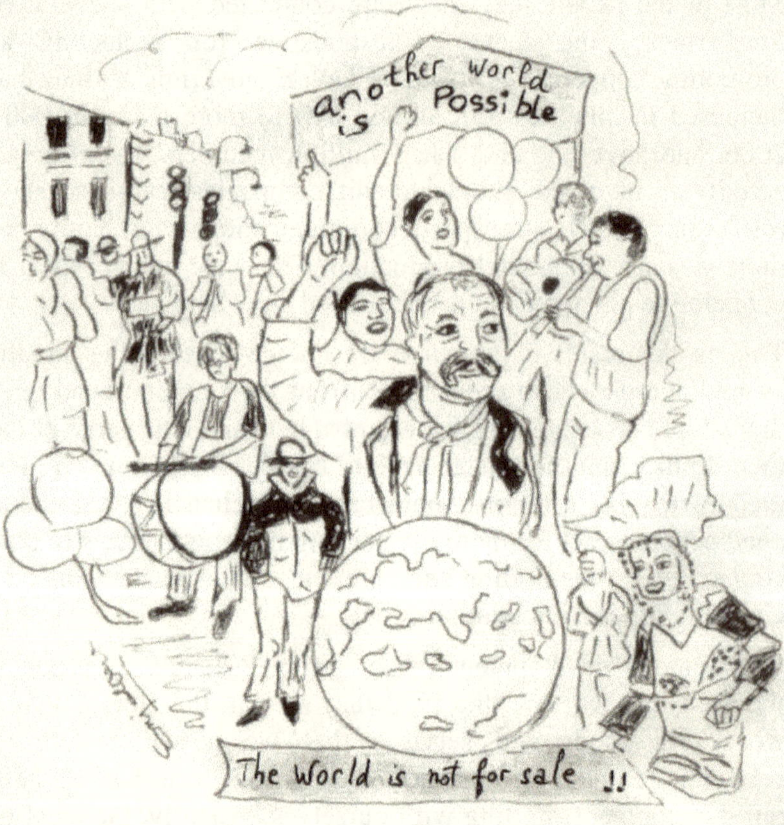
another world is Possible
The World is not for sale !!

The 1999 demonstrations in Seattle to protest against relinquishing global society to the unchecked control of universal capitalism were a true sign of growing awareness. Since then, the many movements (there were at least 800 different groups in

Seattle) have become aware of their emergence and their common purpose.

The worldwide movement for social change has given birth to a remarkable institution in the shape of world social forums. The first Forum was held in January 2001 in Porto Alegre in Brazil, and since then, the event is regularly repeated in different parts of the world. It is interesting to observe the extent to which mainstream media treat it with discretion, although as the new millennium dawned, this was almost certainly the most significant event. It was intended to take place at the same time as the economic summit in Davos, Switzerland, which gathers together all the authorities of the old order, and which the world Forum opposes on every issue.

The World Social Forum brings together hundreds of peoples' movements on a global scale, working to transform society and resolve the world's problems, as made clear by the slogan, "another world is possible".

The aim is to achieve sustainable development and social and economic justice through autonomous and self-generated means – the opposite of neoliberal globalization.

There is a wide variety of organizations and networks taking part and expressing an equally wide variety of perspectives. Not only are there networks of solidarity-based economics and cooperatives, but also NGOs, pacifist movements, movements against the WTO or third world debt, and those working for human rights, workers', women's and children's rights, those trying to solve ecological problems, alternative media, and organizations for basic development requirements as well as ethical consumerism, microfinance and many others.

The truly global nature of the movement is underscored by the fact that it not bound by any political, religious or ideological affiliations. Its thinking makes a clean slate of everything that previously existed, and really starts from scratch in a universal way.

Changing the world means calling everything into question, and this is why the movement encompasses such great diversity, addressing and accepting all aspects of society. It is almost impossible for us to imagine the new world which could arise from this.

Its diversity is not a weakness which will cause the movement to break up – it is a force moving forward on every front. There will be countless disagreements, divisions and failures, but these will help discard solutions which do not work and invent others. There is no constrictive formal relationship to hamper or stifle inventiveness; networks are autonomous and changing – they can die off or be transformed or reborn.

The World Social Forum Charter of Principles clearly establishes its goal which is to oppose neoliberalism and the world's domination by capitalism or any other form of imperialism.

Has the world ever experienced a time of such significance?

Recreating a planetary society built on positive foundations is, as the text states, "a new stage in world history."

> "Founding society on democratic international systems, in opposition to globalization run by multinational corporations as well as social control through violence, respecting human rights and authentic democracy, and promoting relationships of peace and solidarity between all peoples."

15. Solidarity Economics

The solidarity economics movement defines its motivations and aims very clearly:

> "Why produce only as a function of an unjust market that depletes and exploits, denying us the chance to manage both the production and the economy for our own service, for the service of all citizens, and of all peoples of the planet, as well as for future generations?
>
> Why remain subordinated to the will of transnational corporations, States, and international institutions that identify themselves with exclusionary interests, if together, with our collective force, we can create public spaces, states, and new organizations that serve society's empowerment, so that it becomes the leading subject of its own development in an autonomous and self-reliant way?
>
> Why not become subjects of a creative and satisfactory work, free from oppression and exploitation, and which produces what we lack in order to meet our needs—cultural, physical, spiritual, emotional, and relational?
>
> Our proposal is a socioeconomy of solidarity as a way of life that encompasses the totality of the human being, that announces a new culture and a new form of producing to fulfill the needs of each human being and of the entire humanity."

This passage is from a meeting on a Culture and Socioeconomy of Solidarity in Porto Alegre, Brazil, in August 1998, and is quoted in *Solidarity Economics*. (1)

Instead of individuals or groups seeking to expand develop indefinitely their personal advantage through unbridled competition and constant growth, solidarity economics turns the situation upside down. Goals are no longer defined by money, and priority is no longer given to making a profit for a small, exclusive group; on the contrary, the aim is to fulfill people's needs, everyone's, if possible, via networks of generalized cooperation.

This is a Copernican revolution involving a qualitative leap which testifies to a growing moral awareness. Deciding to go from dependence to autonomy, from exclusion to independent integration, means transforming not only working conditions but also how we all relate to everyone involved, and therefore transforming the social environment by adopting new values. The solidarity movement does not mean depriving oneself of one's personal advantages for the benefit of an anonymous community but instead extending limited self-interest to encompass a larger whole. It involves exceeding the limitations of one's blind spot to see the bigger picture and seeing one's self-interest as part of the good of the community. It means forgetting one's obsession with personal greed. It is a moral revolution.

In the article quoted above (*"Solidarity Economics"*), Ethan Miller writes:

> "Through solidarity, we recognize the diversity, autonomy, power, and dignity of others. We come to understand that our struggles to be free and joyful are not as separate or distant from one another as we may have thought. We begin to develop an ethical practice of shared struggle.
>
> Solidarity, then, is a practice of fostering these and other related values with our fellow humans (social and

economic solidarity) and with the rest of the Earth (ecological solidarity):

- Unity-in-diversity
- Shared power (as opposed to power-over)
- Autonomy (both individual and collective)
- Communication (horizontal, not top-down)
- Cooperation and mutual-aid (shared struggle)
- Local rootedness, global inter-connection."

And again:

"Solidarity economics is an organizing tool that can be used to re-value and make connections between the practices of cooperation, mutual aid, reciprocity, and generosity that already exist in our midst. Such a tool can work to encourage collective processes of building diverse, locally-rooted and globally-connected, ecologically-sound, and directly democratic economies outside the control of either the capitalist Market or the State...

...When someone asks the big question, "so what's the alternative?", solidarity economics answers not with a Big Scheme (a "third way" beyond the Market or the State), but with another question: By what means, on whose terms, and with what guiding ethical principles will we collectively work towards new economic structures and relationships? This is an economic process, not a plan; it is a strategy for economic organizing that starts with our already-present practices..."

In their article entitled *"Cooperativization as Alternative to Globalizing Capitalism"* (2), Betsy Bowman and Bob Stone write:

"Cooperativization shifts the basic priority of society's productive infrastructure from profits to needs [...] Initially the needs a co-op serves are those of its own worker-members [...] In shifting to need, the heart of an enterprise shifts from an amoral to a moral bond. For in creating a co-op, each member gives their labor power to the others with a view to meeting the needs of all members, including oneself."

We have already seen how transformations in global society occur along the same lines as the natural evolution of living systems and there is nothing surprising about this. The life all around us is organized into multiple systems which exist throughout nature. The body is a good example; from individual cells, the body's organs, various tissues, the whole body – all these tiers make up an organization of superimposed systems which, while being autonomous are also interdependent, and function in intrinsic harmony. The various social organs - families as well as businesses – also represent systems, in other words, entities which exist through their own particular characteristics, but also through the relationships which unite them with their surroundings. It's easy to see that the body's organs are both autonomous and interdependent, alive in themselves and in the connections which bind them with the other organs whose functioning they also contribute to. The important thing is the network of relationships uniting them. The systems, when grouped together, (a human being, for example) make up a whole, which is greater than the sum of its parts.

One of living systems' essential characteristics is that they are organized in an autonomous fashion, defining their own structure and function, and can renew themselves in order to stay alive; they can also exceed their limitations to develop and evolve further.

Polanyi, (quoted by David Loy in "*Religion and the Market*") (3) observes that when capitalism reduced labor to a commodity, on the one hand, it led to a fantastic accumulation of capital, and on the other, a radical collapse of traditional community life, as the new economic forces drove villagers off their land.

"To separate labor from other activities of life and to subject it to the laws of the market was to annihilate all organic forms of existence and to replace them by a

> different type of organization, an atomistic and individualistic one." Such a system would very soon "annihilate the human and natural substance of society."

But it is precisely this human and natural substance of society that solidarity economics has started to recreate by repairing the breakdown caused by market economy.

These bonds of solidarity - ethical and human bonds - will recreate global society along new lines.

> "Solidarity economics pursues a dynamic process of economic organizing in which organizations, communities, and social movements work to identify, strengthen, connect, and create democratic and liberatory means of meeting their needs
>
> At its core, solidarity economics rejects one-size-fits-all solutions and singular economic blueprints, embracing instead a view that economic and social development

should occur from the bottom up, diversely and creatively crafted by those who are most affected," writes Ethan Miller in his article "*Other Economies Are Possible*" (4)

Ana Mercedes Sarria Icaza, a Brazilian activist, also quoted in this article, states:

> "To speak of a solidarity economy is not to speak of a homogeneous universe with similar characteristics. Indeed, the universe of the solidarity economy reflects a multiplicity of spaces and forms, as much in what we would call the 'formal aspects' (size, structure, governance) as in qualitative aspects (levels of solidarity, democracy, dynamism, and self-management)."

"*Other Economies Are Possible*" also cites Marcos Arruda of the Brazilian Solidarity Economy Network, who declared at the World Social Forum in 2004:

> "A solidarity economy does not arise from thinkers or ideas; it is the outcome of the concrete historical struggle of the human being to live and to develop him/herself as an individual and a collective [...] Innovative practices at the micro level can only be viable and structurally effective for social change if they interweave with one another to form always-broader collaborative networks and solidarity chains of production-finance-distribution-consumption-education-communication."

The active cooperation of diverse organizations which share the same values and mutually reinforce each other is the cornerstone of solidarity economics, representing a re-founding of society which goes beyond the economic level, continually joining up with other essential human activities - the fabric of social relationships, education, communication and higher development – the very concerns which had been wiped out by the arrival of modern capitalism.

Those involved in solidarity economics are well aware that they're opening up the way to changing the world with changes that have already been occurring for a long time, smoothly and naturally. Substantial networks exist in numerous countries (Spain, Brazil, Venezuela, Colombia, Argentina and many others). Other, varied experiments, both new and very old, are taking place almost everywhere.

In *The Turning Point*, F. Capra also notes (in Chapter 12) that citizen and consumer movements have resulted in alternative economies founded on lifestyles which are decentralized, cooperative and ecologically sound, and which are based on exchanging skills, goods and domestic services. These alternative economies are not programmed or established by those in power (from the top down), but are set up spontaneously and develop through experience. They have sprung up in the US, Canada, the UK, Scandinavia, Holland, Japan, Australia and New Zealand.

This may still seem pretty modest; even in Venezuela, the most resolute country, where solidarity economics represents only 5% of the work-force. There are other, more encouraging figures...the International Cooperative Alliance describes itself thus:

"Founded in 1895, the International Co-operative Alliance is ...the largest non-governmental organization in the world. The ICA currently has 221 member organizations from 85 countries in every sector of the economy, representing some 800 million individuals worldwide." That's 800 million members and 100 million workers world-wide.

Obviously, this represents only a small fraction of the global economy, but mighty trees grow from tiny seeds, and the movement will probably have to progress over several centuries. The important thing is that it's on the right path. The journey of a thousand leagues begins with a single step, and that step has already been taken.

16. Entrepreneurial Concepts

The core problem in economics is the sharing of profits. We now live according to the "Law of the Market", in other words, the survival of the fittest, and this has led us to an impasse which is as much economic as it is ethical. It is crucial that we reach a state where the law of the most just, the most effective and the happiest prevails.

Even though people have gone to great lengths to discredit or ignore Marx' analysis, it nevertheless remains totally valid. It is still true that capitalists possess the means of production, and therefore they are able to pocket profits and determine working conditions. The two parties to the contract, i.e. the employer and the employee, are not in an equal position of power, and consequently, the employer can continue to reap the benefits of the employee's labor, and continue to accumulate wealth. The issue of the sharing of profits remains a fundamental moral problem in society as the acquisition of wealth is established in an exclusive monopoly.

J. W. Smith is a researcher who has presented an extremely pertinent analysis of this point. He shows how over the centuries there has been a constant battle to control the process of the creation of wealth. Our current wars are the most recent example of this. In the Middle Ages, the monopolization of land meant that wealth was concentrated in the hands of the few. Afterwards, the control of wealth has always been achieved by means of monopolization, by which a few lucky chosen ones take possession of what in fact constitutes society's common property. These days, he says, we claim to have eradicated monopolies, but in fact we have done nothing of the sort. Monopolization has become subtle and is part of our legislation. In an invisible yet legal way, a small number of people have kept the exclusive rights (rather like the remnants of feudal laws) over what ought to belong to everyone communally. Legal structures guarantee and perpetuate those privileges.

> "Proponents of the current excessive rights structured into law fail to understand that giving a few an excessive share of rights restricts the rights of others (inequality structured in law) and thus is a subtle form of monopolization." (1)

The community's rights are ignored in title deeds to Nature's riches. These rights ought to be reestablished in the form of modern 'commons' (community property) with regards to the riches of the soil, the use of technology, access to financial capital, created wealth, the right to information and the share of the profit from these assets. All of these areas are means of creating wealth which have been subtly monopolized. This instructive viewpoint makes it clear that legal structures give capitalists a huge and unfair advantage.

J. W. Smith suggests precise and detailed ways to carry out his social revolution, but we are not ready for this yet. Firstly, the fact that the power and information are still in the hands of the privileged few means that change is not possible in the foreseeable future. Nevertheless, we cannot rule out the possibility that over the next few centuries, society will evolve enough to achieve what he suggests and his ideas will still be entirely valid. We also know that reform founded upon abstract ideas and springing up out of the blue as a 'Deus ex machina' can only end in disastrous failure. On the contrary, we should trust in society to evolve organically and naturally, just as a living system does.

Can capitalism be reformed?

While the system pursues its excesses until it makes itself sick, at the same time we can see the efforts capitalism is making to clean up its act.

Numerous learned studies have been carried out into entrepreneurial ethics, but the result has simply led to a code of conduct to ensure that companies act as good citizens, mainly in respecting the human rights of employees and stakeholders, as well as respecting the environment. It remains within the legal framework of capitalism as it currently exists.

In the same way, many schemes to share profits or award bonuses or shares depending on profits have been in existence for a long time, and this system is advantageous for both parties.

There are also practical measures such as the Social Venture Network (2). This is network of companies in various countries which have committed themselves to acting in a socially and ecologically responsible manner.

Even though this represents a great leap forward, progress is not radical and this does not alter the crucial problem - the relationship between capital and labor. For real change to occur, the current legal structures have to be modified in order to instill deeply ethical relationships which transcend businesses' good intentions and reach a more spiritual level. Reaching a deeply ethical level means managing to achieve fairness in the sharing of profit.

Is it possible to imagine a balanced form of capitalism?

Some companies which provide jobs and pay a decent wage would have to close shop if they were forced to do even better.

But in prosperous companies, employees remain in an archaic situation:

> "Workers have no choice but to rent out the strength of their arms and the intelligence of their brains to those who have capital. Capital does not produce anything, it simply buys creative ability." (3)

It is said that in business, each person receives their share depending on what they bring to the company, but this share is very difficult to evaluate. We should bear in mind that it is not capital that creates wealth, but labor. Capital plays a passive role – we could call it 'inert capital' - while labor could be considered as 'active capital', without which nothing could be created. Obviously, inert capital can create the conditions for a company to exist, but it is unjust that inert capital should have an excessive advantage over active capital. Labor is not a commodity; it is act of creation.

Consequently, it is wholly justified that labor's role in the running of a company be at least equal to that of capital, and as part of its management role, it should have its say about the sharing of profits and in determining company policies.

> "Capital does not generate value in itself, and can only grow if it is valorized by productive labor. Yield from capital is therefore always taken from the value created by the workers." (4)

Under these conditions, it would be very tempting to define the balance between active and inert capital as an agreed minimum percentage of capital appreciation - let's say a percentage comparable to bond yields, and maybe a little more in good years. The appreciation of wages would no longer be curbed or cut and would reach a very comfortable level.

It can be assumed that this regime would put an end to the abuses of the system and instill a healthier atmosphere such as we have never experienced. In a collaboratively-managed company such as this, workers would be integrated in their rightful capacity and feel themselves to be part of their meaningful work. They would experience better job security and would naturally be productive and creative. They would find themselves in a legitimate, fair and humane environment. Society would be totally transformed.

We could even speculate that this would be good for the Stock Exchange as it could promise more limited but more secure and permanent yields.

Studies into finding solutions to replace capitalism generally settle on a democratic, participatory, solidarity-based, self-managed economy. (5)

Basic facts

But now let's leave our imaginative reflections and turn our attention towards actual developments.

As we have seen, the most advanced solution has naturally arisen where problems were so acute that the situation had to resolve itself. This is how the cooperative movement was born, and it remains the best solution by a long way.

Betsy Bowman and Bob Stone have written an essay which ought to become one of the new books of the Bible for modern times – "*Cooperativization as Alternative to Globalizing Capitalism*" Geo, October 2005. (6)

Using Mondragon as an example, their realistic and soundly-documented study shows that cooperativization constitutes the ideal remedy for the ills of this world.

With 30,000 employees and $5 billion in annual turnover, the Spanish cooperative of Mondragon remains the most impressive success story in this field. Here are a few extracts from their arguments:

> "Can we construct a better world than that of globalizing capitalism? Yes! Through cooperativization. We claim that first-world networks of worker co-ops - like the one around Mondragon, Spain - if re-oriented so as to solidarize with the alter-globalization movement, could almost fully replace capitalism by a democratic economy [...]
>
> "Productivity and profitability are higher for co-operatives than for capitalist firms [...] Studies of job creation, worker compensation, and job security yield similar results [...]
>
> The productivity advantage of democratic production stimulates cooperativization. This advantage is likely due to harmonizing of conflicting imperatives. Absent rewards, workers in capitalist firms withhold their skills. By contrast workers in democratic firms, no longer pitted against each other, have strong incentives to share skills. And since

> effectively exercising collective creativity is pleasurable, management supervision is less necessary, a big savings. Also lifted is the even greater burden of supporting absentee shareholders. Co-ops thus have a flexibility, financial buoyancy and re-investment potential lacking capitalist firms. Members are not resentfully slow, care for equipment, avoid waste, and minimize downtime and absenteeism. Large-scale production still needs skilled managers, but direct market feedback, freed of "noise" from managers with inimical interests, allows faster remedy of management errors [...]
>
> Usually "profit" is income after all costs, including labor costs [...] Labor is not a "cost" in a co-op but a mutual sharing of each member's capital. Labor time is neither bought nor sold. Rather, a co-op's workers together share all profits and losses [...]
>
> A Mondragon-like co-op re-unites in one person the functions of worker, manager and owner. Capitalism consigns these functions to three separate persons [...]To personify these functions is to impose on the three groups that are thereby constituted an imperative that pits each of them against the other two [...] To then re-unite these functions in each member -- as happens in true worker cooperatives -- necessarily abolishes the conflict among the three groups [...]"

The cooperative system appears to be the most radical and effective system to enable individuals to control their economic destiny, to eradicate exploitation and establish a truly democratic and solidarity-based economy. This would represent total regeneration for social relationships and the birth of a new society in which individuals' aspirations to justice, security and morality could be achieved. Another world is possible.

Workers are realizing that it is their labor and not capital which generates profit, and consequently, there is no need to comply with capital's conditions in order to earn one's living. Cooperatives anchor jobs, and are freed from the demands of absentee shareholders who steal all the profits. They can change the face of the world.

Cooperatives are already a well-established and significant presence in the economic landscape. In the Emilia-Romagna region in Italy, cooperatives of various sizes employ up to 250,000 people. (7)

In Spain and Italy, cooperatives enjoy the official support of the State as they provide jobs.

Betsy Bowman and Bob Stone point out that Europe generally is having a worker co-op boom. There are up to 83,000 companies of this kind in 42 countries, providing 1.3 million jobs - twice as many as 20 years ago. There are cooperative networks in Japan, Canada, Argentina, Brazil, Columbia, Venezuela etc.

Earlier successful experiences in self-management were carried out in Yugoslavia, which inspired others in European countries such as Sweden and Germany. Most industrialized countries have carried out experiments in self-management and workers' participation.

While a cooperative economy is still only a drop in the ocean, it is more significant when seen in the context of the whole group of non-capitalist forms of economy, which includes the examples of solidarity-based economies in Alterglobalism, the local community economies of the Third World, informal exchange economies and, above all, the kinds of companies which are open to workers'participation.

Community and solidarity-based economic models existed in the Soviet Union and China; those countries could have provided a fertile ground where new companies could have started up again on a cooperative and democratic basis. This would have enabled them to avoid an unnecessary detour down the capitalist path which creates as many problems as it solves. It would also vindicate the earnest efforts of those who gave so much or who sacrificed themselves in vain during the era of totalitarian communism.

World solidarity movements are proof that human awareness is evolving and this will have to continue until a fair economy is established everywhere. It is as though the miserable masses appeared in order to force this change to come about.

The autonomous and independent economy is still insignificant in terms of figures on a worldwide scale, but it is extremely significant in other ways. It will act as a catalyst for change. As it develops and succeeds, hardcore neoliberalism will be increasingly affected. Awareness is evolving.

Both global problems and the upsurge in change brought about by fair economics will lead to workers thinking twice about their working conditions, and no longer begging for work nor accepting unsatisfactory working conditions, but instead creating their own jobs within a solidarity-based community.

Change can only occur within each individual and through each and every individual. Changes will follow on each time people create a company along cooperative or democratic lines, or each time an existing company turns into a solidarity-based company.

In the meantime, we should take capitalism at its word and allow companies which are run according to new standards to enter into the game of free, peaceful competition.

May the best man win!!

17. Balance Is Well-Being

Taking Stock

All the misfortune from which the world suffers - poverty, overpopulation, underdevelopment, the damage wreaked upon the environment and social tension – originates from within mankind. All human activity is driven by the instinct to survive, forcing us to adapt as best we can in a hostile - or at least difficult - world. However, our activity creates havoc. We are not merely ensuring our own prosperity and safety – we are doing so in ways which mean we are heading for disaster. Most of us have no control over how things are done, nor any choice. In the current world order, we are driven to struggle for survival as best we can, fighting amongst ourselves to gain any possible advantage. Humankind and the turmoil we generate become an ever-expanding feverish mass, propelled towards unlimited and destructive growth.

Our natural self-centeredness, acts as a pair of opaque glasses, blinding us to the ways in which we are destroying the delicate balance of the Earth, as well as that of our souls.

We are living by principles which cannot but create permanent inequalities, which can only worsen social divisions, personal frustration and the absence of meaning for our existence. The world we have created matches the level of our evolution. Our behavior is centered upon individual motives, without a broader outlook, without a vision of the whole – it is immature behavior, lacking in spiritual development.

Economy is divorced from morality, although the fabric deep within us is woven from morality. In this material world were we live, nothing which can be done or thought by a human being may be dissociated in any way from its moral aspect. Our moral nature is not a merely an accessory, or a cultural coloring – it is part of our very nature – and not our intellectual, emotional or mental nature, but rather our more essential and profound being, our intangible, spiritual nature – the nature about which we know nothing, but which is always present, silently observing everything.

Addressing moral or spiritual development does not mean setting off on a quest for the Law of the Twelve Tables or the Ten Commandments. It is simply living according to the spontaneous behavior of a person bent on achieving oneself, setting and reaching one's own standards within oneself. Being in touch with one's spirituality does not imply being enslaved – it is liberation.

Man believes himself to be complete, but he is not. We are imperfect beings who must continue to evolve. Believing oneself to be complete is a form of blindness stemming from self-centeredness.

Living creatures' hunger to survive is channeled entirely into the pursuit of riches, as if money were an essential energy, allowing us not only to live, but also to survive, to prolong our lives, to bolster ourselves. This is a mistake. Money certainly provides a form of energy, but it does not give us the progress we need. Without dismissing prosperity, there are other, more subtle energies to capture which will take us further in our development.

Our activities are not as natural as we might think. Nature detests all that is excessive or deviant. We find ourselves in a situation where our positive evolution is blocked. That situation shapes the structure of society, it shapes the structure of business, it shapes our mental structures, and it shapes our world. We neither know how to create a common, accepted aim for a satisfactory, fair, balanced, clean, happy, sustainable and harmonious society, nor how to acquire the means to do so.

Looking Towards the Future

Those observations about our past can be understood by anyone. Now we must look towards the future in order better to determine which path to take.

We have raised the question of how to resolve the problems of the world which are connected to the economy.

The answer that we come up with is that those problems can only be resolved by developing our individual conscience. Evolution occurs on a personal and conscious level. This enables us to tackle the conditions of economic activity in a spirit of fairness and freedom. The solution can only be found along the path of liberation, the path of autonomy and responsibility, in other words, the freedom of each person in his work. While one person remains oppressed or precarious in his or her material resources, this has not been accomplished. The first step towards the joy of living and quality of life lies in equal prosperity for everyone. It is up to us to act; up to those of us who are suffering to undertake these changes. When the spirit evolves, practical solutions may then be found.

.

We have recently observed that perfectly adapted responses have begun to emerge, and this is very encouraging – there has been an evolution in perceptions and a new form of adaptation. This is particularly true of the principle of solidarity-based economy, which is not sentimental philanthropy, nor simply an appeal for voluntary self-sacrifice, but rather an understanding that it is in everyone's best interests.

The solution gives us the capacity to take our destiny into our own hands, making us independent and responsible both towards ourselves and others. Economic activity is moving onto a different level, becoming part of a vision with a broader conscience.

Work becomes a commitment which has meaning. It is gratifying.

Solidarity becomes an invisible thread restoring social relationships.

Precariousness is eradicated, the environment is respected, and the face of the Earth is changed.

Personal and spiritual relationships once again take pride of place, allowing us to continue to develop in a wholesome way.

One day we shall come to understand that activity does not mean making money or accumulating wealth, but creating goods and services to fulfill all our needs, and working with others for others as well as ourselves.

One day we shall come to understand that the fundamental rule for activity to generate a better quality of life is the rule of striking a happy balance.

This touches upon what we mean by 'good practice', which is both subjective and objective. It is, first of all, a subjective process, making us realize what striking a happy balance actually is, what a just decision is, and what we mean by just and optimal. This decision springs from the profound roots of our soul, from the silent observer in the depths of every conscience.

Then, external proof with external aims will follow. The best kind of satisfaction is not maximal satisfaction (which is an illusory and contradictory concept), beyond which we trip up and out troubles really begin, as we all know.

Happiness established in solidarity and cooperation is profound and enriching. It opens up to others; it opens up one's conscience and becomes happiness based on trust, giving access to more profound, more sustainable, truer perspectives. This is why achieving true well-being may be defined as what enables real human development.

Economic activity is no longer, then, the only measure. The notion of "increased GDP = higher standard of living = development" is unsatisfactory. The growth of GDP linked to the growth of the masses is distension, it is the same as getting bloated or a destructive swelling – it is not development worthy of our human potential.

A coyote catches a rabbit, eats it and then sleeps it off. It wishes for nothing more. Human activity is vaster. You get your paycheck, you pay your bills, you satisfy all your requirements, you put a bit aside for your projects, you even take a vacation, spend a little on leisure activities – and then? Something is still missing, after all that, unless you see existence as merely spending time going round and round on a roundabout. That is not what will give your life a meaning.

After spending some enjoyable time with friends, we're fully satisfied; life has meaning because we have increased our quality of life, and experienced well-being.

However, there are other requirements for personal achievement which go even further than that.

Determining our Path

Determining the path that our activity should take is not difficult – it merely involves formulating what each one of us desires.

Isn't it obvious that humanity's sole aim should be for the best possible quality of life? In other words, generalized and universal well-being. This does not mean that we can eliminate all life's problems. This earthly existence can never be without obstacles and problems. Difficulties, catastrophes, frustration and contradictions are an inherent part of life. They are structurally established, and part of the immovable architecture, whether we like it or not. We are creatures amongst all the others. We inhabit the world, but it was not created especially for us. The quest for harmony inevitably drives humanity to rise above the conditions of its existence.

Personal evolution is the key to the world's salvation. This occurs naturally with the evolution of the collective conscience, but ancient traditional methods of personal development such as meditation may also provide crucial support. Simply practicing energetic, gentle gymnastic techniques such as Yoga or Qigong can result in profound personal fulfillment; they enable us to draw what we require to progress directly from the surrounding field of energy. They give us the possibility to draw directly the physical, mental and spiritual energy we need to establish sound health and a firm basic happiness, and, in the long term, to advance along the path of our evolution which consists of further awakening our conscience.

Quality of life - generalized, universal, material and psychic well-being – is technically achievable, even if we must be prepared for slow, secular progression.

Where are we now?

A possible answer may be found in an article on the emergence of a new, planetary democratic movement (*"A global Democratic Movement is About to Pop"*). (1)

> "It will be the stroke of midnight for the rest of our lives. It is too late for heroes. We need an accelerated intertwining of the over 1 million nonprofits and 100 million people who daily work for the preservation and restoration of life on earth. ...The language of sustainability is about ideas that never end: growth without inequality, wealth without plunder, work without exploitation, a future without fear. A green movement fails unless there's a black-, brown-, and copper-colored movement, and that can only exist if the movement to change the world touches the needs and suffering of every single person on earth."
>
> -- *Worldchanging.org* 12/26/06. Paul Hawken.

While he was on tour, giving conferences on the environment, Paul Hawken was constantly being contacted by nonprofit organizations and NGOs committed to protecting the environment and social reform. He realized that he had gathered several thousand contacts of this kind over the years.

So he decided to calculate how many organizations there could be working to change the world and came to the conclusion that there were over a million, maybe two million. And this is significant – such a major phenomenon is hidden from us by the media which supposedly informs us.

He saw that it was not a movement led by leaders or ideologies, but rather an organic reaction to the earth's disease. This recalls the reflections made on the evolution and adaptation of ecosystems. The movement is independent and autonomous; it has no name; it is dispersed yet connected, and is probably the biggest social movement in history. It involves tens of millions of ordinary citizens working against the odds to give a little harmony, justice and beauty back to our world.

Paul Hawken writes:

> "The movement grows and spreads in every city and country. Virtually every tribe, culture, language, and religion is part of it, from Mongolians to Uzbeks to Tamils. It is comprised of families in India, students in Australia, farmers in France, the landless in Brazil, the bananeras of Honduras, the "poors" of Durban, villagers in Irian Jaya, indigenous tribes of Bolivia, and housewives in Japan [...]
>
> The movement has three basic roots: the environmental and social justice movements, and indigenous cultures' resistance to globalization [...] the very word movement may be too small, for it is the largest coming together of citizens in history [...] And it is impossible to pin down [...]
>
> The movement does not agree on everything nor will it ever, because that would be an ideology. But it shares a basic set of fundamental understandings about the Earth, how it functions, and the necessity of fairness and equity for all people partaking of the planet's life-giving systems. The promise of this unnamed movement is to offer solutions to what appear to be insoluble dilemmas: poverty, global climate change, terrorism, ecological degradation, polarization of income, loss of culture. It is not burdened with a syndrome of trying to save the world; it is trying to remake the world [...]
>
> There is fierceness here. There is no other explanation for the raw courage and heart seen over and again in the people who march, speak, create, resist, and build. It is the fierceness of what it means to know we are human and want to survive.

This movement is relentless and unafraid. It cannot be mollified, pacified, or suppressed [...] The movement will continue to take myriad forms. It will not rest [...] the movement is the breathing, sentient testament of the living world [...]

The thinking that informs the movement's goal -- to create a just society conducive to life on Earth -- will reign. It will soon suffuse and permeate most institutions. But before then, it will change a sufficient number of people so as to begin the reversal of centuries of frenzied self-destruction.

Inspiration is not garnered from litanies of what is flawed; it resides in humanity's willingness to restore, redress, reform, recover, reimagine, and reconsider. Healing the wounds of the Earth and its people does not require saintliness or a political party. It is not a liberal or conservative activity. It is a sacred act."

Let's enjoy ourselves!

Let's take a moment to enjoy ourselves imagining this Utopian world which is not yet born, but which is entirely within our reach, if we could only realize it.

We can see a new world appearing.

Let's visualize the radiant future which we have the means to achieve; a world where everyone has enough to eat; a world where the most advanced knowledge is evenly distributed; a world where prosperity is a fundamental reality for everyone. Let's say that means on average € 50,000 for everyone who has a job, as well as two homes, two clean cars and two children, on average, more or less. Ugly districts have disappeared. Large cities, healthy and well-spaced out, medium-sized towns, villages and countryside, all stabilized at the optimal point of development, which may be subject to fluctuations. Cities have stopped sprawling, many of them have shrunk, and all of them breathe. Everyone who wants a garden has one. The wretched masses no longer exist. Human creatures are active without being frantic, working together in warm, spontaneous harmony. Humankind has rediscovered transparency and life once again has meaning.

There is no longer unrest in the workplace – cooperation and emulation have replaced destructive competitiveness. Profits remain within the business, representing the flame of happiness, reward, a guarantee of success and continuity. Solidarity-based businesses have dealings in symbiosis, like cells from a single, universal organism.

We will see a surge in unharmful growth, based upon self-interest but nonetheless rooted in solidarity too. Nothing prevents a way of a life where knowledge improves and brilliant discoveries continue, and where the standard of living, comfort and wealth increase significantly without causing disruption.

The environment is protected and can regenerate itself, regaining its original sustainable permanence which ancient peoples preserved religiously. Population fluctuates freely, but is no longer forced into frenzied development in response to the ambitions of the major economic, social and political players. It finds its own optimal level for everyone to live and move about without any difficulty whatsoever, even to park a car – now that really is progress!

At the same time, healthy, appreciative relations between people are established - relations of trust where aggression has evaporated; festive, spontaneous relations; a new way of life giving rise to new human accomplishments; a quest to deepen the meaning of life and personal development; a quest for true well-being which does not destroy nature.

And each of us should add whatever's missing! In this way we'll have envisaged, at least once, the new world which we haven't yet been able to create.

In reality, we cannot know what the new world will be like. As yet, it is uncertain. But from this moment on, each of our thoughts, our decisions and our orientations will imperceptibly contribute to making it materialize.

After a period of wisdom and innocence (which can still be seen in some primitive peoples,) humanity lost its way in youthful distractions. Like so many pleasure-seeking smart kids, humanity almost lost its soul and almost ceased to survive. It is time to take the management of our destiny in hand and stop believing in myths forged by those who are the only ones to profit from them. It is time to see that our society is a free-for-all rat race, and unworthy of us.

It is time to recognize that material values and moral, spiritual values are inextricably linked, and all elements of the same reality. It is time to recognize that it's moral values which should be guiding our evolution. It is time to appeal to enlightened individual consciences, rather than just ignorant self-interest as before.

The road will be long, but there is no other way.

Our emancipation will be achieved through the individual progress of our consciences together with external economic structures which are fair and balanced.

As a first step forward, the way for humanity consists in achieving material liberation. If we manage to attain this liberation, the path to a beautiful future will be guaranteed for the rest of our human journey.

End of Part I

Sources and Documents

Chapter 1. A Quick Glance at the Planet.

(1) Mila Kahlon. Une obsession nommée Bombay.

http://www.monde-diplomatique.fr/2004/01/KHALON/10659

(2) http://www.globalissues.org

(3) Quoted in the article by R. Bleier *Feeding the Population Monster*, about a book by M. Tobias.

http://desip.igc.org/Monster.html

No Tears for Theogen. http://www.newint.org/issue285/tears.htm

Brazil- Poorer 25 years later.

www.brazzil.com/2004/html/articles/jun04/p102jun04.htm

Rio de Janeiro, Many Cities in One. The favelas,

http://www.macalester.edu/courses/geog61/chad/thefavel.htm

Chapter 2. Neoliberalism.

(1) A Primer on Neoliberalism.

http://www.globalissues.org/TradeRelated/FreeTrade/Neoliberalism.asp

(2) What is Neoliberalism?

http://www.corpwatch.org/article.php?id=376

(3) Criticisms of Current Forms of Free Trade.

http://www.globalissues.org/TradeRelated/FreeTrade/Criticisms.asp

Can Radical Capitalism Survive the Disasters It Creates?

http://www.alternet.org/workplace/63288/

Global Problems and the Culture of Capitalism.

http://faculty.plattsburgh.edu/richard.robbins/legacy/global.htm

Comment l'AMI fut mis en pièces.

http://www.monde-diplomatique.fr/1998/12/DE_BRIE/11435.html

The essence of neoliberalism.

http://www.monde-diplomatique.fr/1998/03/BOURDIEU/10167

Chapter 3. A Quick Glance at Developed Countries.

(1) OECD study highlights widespread and persistent poverty in Europe and America, http://www.wsws.org/articles/2000/feb2000/pov-f04.shtml

(2) S.Wheelan. The Brazilianisation of Britain's Cities.

http://www.wsws.org/articles/1999/jul1999/ubn-j28.shtml

(3) Hunger and Poverty in the United States.

http://www.results.org/website/article.asp?id=350

(4) Ben H. Bagdikian. A Secret in the News: The Country's Permanent Poor.

http://lookingglassnews.org/printerfriendly.php?storyid=2083

(5) Wealth Inequality by the Numbers.

http://www.dollarsandsense.org/archives/2004/0104inequality.pdf

(6) C. Collins and F. Yeskel. Billionaires R Us. http://www.alternet.org/workplace/27168

(7) B. Ehrenreich. It's the (Tanking) Economy, Stupid.

http://www.alternet.org/story/41533/

(8) M. Lanzarotta. The Wealth Gap Challenges American Ideals.

http://www.impactpress.com/articles/augsep01/divide80901.html

(9) R. Teixeira. The Myth of the Investor Class.

http://www.prospect.org/cs/articles?article=the_myth_of_the_investor_class

Oxfam, Poverty in the UK,
http://www.oxfam.org.uk/resources/ukpoverty/povertyfacts.html

In egalitarian Europe, a not-so-hidden world of squalor,
http://www.iht.com/articles/2005/10/17/news/housing.php

Profits Before People. The Income Gap.
http://www.workplacefairness.org/sc/incomegap.php

Chapter 4. A United World for Better or for Worse.

(1) World Poverty has Declined Sharply Under Globalization.
http://www.iie.com/publications/newsreleases/newsrelease.cfm?id=83

(2) D. Jesuit and T. Smeeding. Poverty Levels in the Developed World.
http://www.lisproject.org/publications/liswps/321.pdf

(3) Mila Kahlon. India's City of Gold.
Le Monde diplomatique, English edition, January 2004.

Chapter 5. The Law of the Market.

(1) David Loy. Religion and the Market.
http://www.religiousconsultation.org/loy.htm

(2) A Buddhist Response to the Age of Globalization
http://go.worldbank.org/0TI83SUG40

(3) R. Kerr. Business Ethics and the Market Economy.
http://www.nzbr.org.nz/documents/speeches/speeches-98/business_ethics_and_the_market_economy.doc.htm

(4) John Ikerd. Rethinking the Economics of Self-Interests.
http://web.missouri.edu/ikerdj/papers/Rethinking.html

Chapter 6. The Quest for the Highest Profit.

(1) David Loy. Religion and the Market. Op.cit.

(2) F. Capra, *The Turning Point* chapter 7.
http://www.wplus.net/pp/Julia/Capra/CONTENTS.htm

(3) Venerable Payutto, *Buddhist Economics*, chapter 2.
http://www.urbandharma.org/udharma2/becono.html

In Greed We Trust, John F. Schumaker
http://www.newint.org/columns/essays/2004/07/01/greed/

The Drive for Profits at Capitalism's core.
http://socialistworker.org/2002-2/429/429_09_Profit.shtml

Chapter 7. Dinosaurs.

(1) http://www.globalissues.org

(2) John Ikerd. Rethinking the Economics of Self-Interests. Op.cit.

(3) F. Capra, *The Turning Point*, chapter 7. Op.cit.

(4) Tax Havens: Releasing the hidden billions for poverty eradication

http://www.oxfam.org.uk

http://www.globalissues.org/article/54/evasion-of-tax-and-other-responsibilities#TransferPricingInterceptingWealth

(5) David Loy. Religion and the Market. Op. cit.

http://www.suisse.attac.org/Paradis-Fiscaux-comment-les-Etats

http://www.oulala.net/Portail/article.php3?id_article=172

Global Policy Forum on Tax Havens

http://www.globalpolicy.org/nations/sovereign/taxindex.htm

Chapter 8. The Growth of the Masses.

Readings on Population

http://faculty.plattsburgh.edu/richard.robbins/legacy/global_problems_reader_frames.htm

Human population. A Numbers Game

http://www.globalissues.org/EnvIssues/Population/Numbers.asp

Chapter 9. A Cancer-like Growth.

(1) R. Bleier. Feeding the Population Monster. Op.cit.

(2) S. Weissman : Marx and Engels on the Population Bomb.
http://www.fortunecity.com/victorian/literary/96/population.html

(3) John Ikerd. Rethinking the Economics of Self-Interests. Op.cit.

(4) Frank Brunner. La Logique interne de l'intérêt général :
http://www.interet-general.info/

http://www.globalissues.org

It's Time to Fight Population Growth, Which Exacerbates Global Warming and Sprawl.
http://www.alternet.org/story/50216/

Chapter 10. A Matter of Conscience.

(1) David Loy. Religion and the Market. Op.cit.

(2) The Human Development concept.

http://hdr.undp.org/en/humandev/

(3) F. Capra, *The Turning Point*, chapter 12. Op.cit.

(4) "*The Wisdom Teachings of the Dalai Lama*," (p.179) Quoted by par John Ikerd in " Rethinking the Economics of Self-Interests," Op.cit.

Chapter 11. The Principles for Change.

(1) Ken Wilber Summary of Spiral Dynamics model
www.satori-5.co.uk/downloads/dlf_159.doc
(2) Spiral Dynamics, a theory of human development.
http://en.wikipedia.org/wiki/Spiral_Dynamics

The Science of Collective Consciousness.
http://www.wie.org/j25/kenny.asp

Global Consciousness Change.
http://www.awakeningearth.org/PDF/global_consciousness.pdf

Chapter 12. For the Happy Few.

(1) Venerable Payutto, *Buddhist Economics*, chapter 5. Op.cit.

http ://www.qigonginstitute.org/html/papers/MeditationBibliography.pdf

Scientific study of meditation :

The Physical and Psychological Effects of Meditation
http://www.noetic.org/research/medbiblio/index.htm

Chapter 13. The Ways In Which Change Is Occurring.

(1) http://www.globalissues.org

(2) John Ikerd. Rethinking the Economics of Self-Interests. Op.cit.

(3) Venerable Payutto, *Buddhist Economics*, chapter 2. Op.cit.

Chapter 14. Observing the Changes.

(1) World Hunger : 12 Myths, quoted in Global Issues in section « Food Dumping [Aid] Maintains Poverty). Op.cit.

(2)
http://www.dollarsandsense.org/archives/2006/0706bowmanstone.html

Susan George: Democracy at the Barricades,
http://mondediplo.com/2001/08/02genoa

B. Bowman and B. Stone on Venezuela's Revolution,
http://www.geonewsletter.org/archives/Bolivar.htm

Chapter 15. Solidarity Economics.

(1) Ethan Miller. Solidarity Economics.
http://www.geonewsletter.org/archives/SolidarityEconomicsEthanMiller.htm

(2) B. Bowman, B Stone, Cooperativization as Alternative to Globalizing Capitalism.

http://www.geonewsletter.org/archives/bowmanstone1104.htm

(3) David Loy. Religion and the Market. Op.cit.

(4) Ethan Miller. Other Economies Are Possible.
http://dollarsandsense.org/archives/2006/0706emiller.html

Hugo Chavez, par Ignacio Ramonet.
http://www.monde-diplomatique.fr/2007/08/RAMONET/15003

America beyond Capitalism, Alperovitz.
http://www.dollarsandsense.org/archives/2004/1104alper.html

Forum social mondial. Porto Alegre 2003.
http://www.france.attac.org/spip.php?rubrique164

Center for Global Justice
http://www.globaljusticecenter.org/indexing.htm

It's Time to Build a New Economic Model. David Korten.
http://www.alternet.org/environment/63019/

Chapter 16. Entrepreneurial Concepts.

(1) J.W. Smith. Cooperative Capitalism. A blueprint for Global Peace and Prosperity.

http://www.ccus.info/books/cc/intro.shtml

(2) The Social Venture Network.

http://www.cauxroundtable.org/SocialVentureNetworkStandardsofCorporateSocialResponsibility.htm

(3) Alternatives Economiques n° 65 - Hors-série - Le Capitalisme- 2005

(4) Fondation Copernic, « Diagnostics pour sortir du libéralisme », p 22

(5) A Comparison of Economic Democracy and Participatory Economics

www.zmag.org/znet/viewArticle/6345

L'entreprise autogérée

http://www.m-lasserre.com/textes/entrepriseautogeree.htm

(6) Cooperativization as Alternative to Globalizing Capitalism.

http://www.geonewsletter.org/node/139

(7) Tim Huet, Can Coops Go Global?

http://www.dollarsandsense.org/archives/1997/1197huet.html

A Statistical Profile of Employee Ownership.

http://www.nceo.org/library/eo_stat.html

Recuperated Enterprises in Argentina.

http://upsidedownworld.org/main/content/view/235/1/

Todor Kuljic. Yugoslavia's workers self-management

http://www.republicart.net/disc/aeas/kuljic01_en.pdf

Chapter 17. Balance Is Well-being.

(1) A Global Democratic Movement Is About to Pop.Paul Hawken, Orion Magazine. Posted May 1, 2007. http://www.alternet.org/environment/51088
Or else:

http://www.igniteall.com/a_global_democratic_movement.pdf

http://www.wiserearth.org/

Printed in France for lulu.com
Other printers for world distribution

Dépôt légal : janvier 2011

www.ingramcontent.com/pod-product-compliance
Lightning Source LLC
La Vergne TN
LVHW091258080426
835510LV00007B/315